PORTFOLIO
ENTREPRENEURSHIP SIMPLIFIED

Ashok Soota is the executive chairman of Happiest Minds Technologies, and was the founding chairman and managing director of MindTree. Prior to MindTree, he led Wipro's IT business for fifteen years. He has been the president of leading industry associations, a member of the prime minister's taskforce for information technology and was on the advisory board of the World Intellectual Property Organization (WIPO). He has a deep interest in entrepreneurship and philanthropy, for which he has founded the SKAN medical research trust and Ashirvadam trust. His hobbies include travel, yoga, tai chi and swimming.

S.R. Gopalan (22 June 1952–15 December 2016) was the founder of Dawn Consulting and Bizworth India, which provide advisory services covering finance, regulation, taxation and strategic aspects of business, as well as the valuation of enterprises and intangibles. Start-ups and early-stage companies constituted a large proportion of his 350 clients. Gopalan was president of TiE Bangalore and served on the boards of several companies. He had a successful corporate career with Union Carbide and Wipro.

ENTREPRENEURSHIP SIMPLIFIED

FROM IDEA TO IPO

ASHOK SOOTA AND S.R. GOPALAN

PORTFOLIO
PENGUIN

An imprint of Penguin Random House

PORTFOLIO

USA | Canada | UK | Ireland | Australia
New Zealand | India | South Africa | China

Portfolio is part of the Penguin Random House group of companies whose
addresses can be found at global.penguinrandomhouse.com

Published by Penguin Random House India Pvt. Ltd
4th Floor, Capital Tower 1, MG Road,
Gurugram 122 002, Haryana, India

Penguin
Random House
India

First published in Portfolio by Penguin Random House India 2016

Copyright © Ashok Soota and S.R. Gopalan 2016, 2021

All rights reserved

10 9 8 7 6 5 4 3 2 1

The views and opinions expressed in this book are the authors' own and the
facts are as reported by them which have been verified to the extent possible,
and the publishers are not in any way liable for the same.

ISBN 9780143454915

Typeset in Minion Pro by Manipal Digital Systems, Manipal
Printed at Replika Press Pvt. Ltd, India

www.penguin.co.in

Ashok Soota dedicates this book
to the three persons who gave him
his career opportunities and from whom
he also learned the most:
the late Dr Charat Ram,
Bishan Sahai
and Azim Premji.

S.R. Gopalan dedicates this book
to his family for their love and support:
his wife, Chandra,
and his sons, Rahul and Siddharth.

Gopalan also dedicates this book to his bosses
who shared their wisdom with him
and were instrumental in his development:
J.H. Sethna, Ashok Soota and Azim Premji.

CONTENTS

Acknowledgements

We would like to acknowledge the contributions made by a wide segment of persons:

First, the serial entrepreneurs K. Ganesh and Alok Mittal who shared deep insights. The many young entrepreneurs who we've assisted and whose real-life issues we've tried to address. The VCs who gave us their perspective: Deepak Kamra of Canaan, Sanjeev Aggarwal of Helion and Sudhir Sethi of IDG. Customers whose perceptions and stories were inspirational: Aref Matin, Deidre Paknad, Gagan Maini, Jayshree Ullal, Mittu Sridhara and Prem Jain. We would also like to thank the *Economic Times* and other media for the extensive coverage they give to entrepreneurship; several of the stories they have published have been included in the book. Also the industry and functional specialists we have quoted, Anup Bagchi of ICICI Securities, Jessie Paul of Paul Writers, Avinash Subramanyam for his contribution to Tai Chi thinking and also Suresh Senapaty.

Thanks are due to colleagues at Happiest Minds whose inputs are quoted: Raja Shanmugam and Gopala Seruku. Also, Rajiv Khaitan, Salil Godika and Davis Karedan for their critiques of specific chapters. Dawn Consulting's Prakash Subramaniam and G. Srinivasan for data research and fact verification. Likewise, Vijay Karthickeyan and Bhoomika Sharma of Welingkar.

ACKNOWLEDGEMENTS

We would like to convey our gratitude to the Penguin team who were a pleasure to work with, particularly Udayan Mitra who was with us through the entire publishing journey.

Finally and most importantly, we would like to acknowledge Ashok's executive assistant (for twenty-three years), Viji, who diligently prepared and checked the different versions of the manuscript. During a brief period when she was indisposed, she made it a family endeavour by enlisting the help of her sister, Girija.

Preface to the Paperback Edition

Four years have flown since Penguin first published *Entrepreneurship Simplified: Idea to IPO*. It has been gratifying to see the book become a national bestseller, with significant number of copies also sold overseas. As we prepare to publish the paperback version of *Entrepreneurship Simplified*, I feel a great sense of nostalgia and sadness. Four weeks after we launched *Entrepreneurship Simplified*, my co-author, S.R. Gopalan, passed away.

Gopalan was my colleague, dear friend and trusted adviser for over thirty years. Ironically, in 2012 both of us had been diagnosed with different cancers within weeks of each other. Both of us faced the prospect of lifestyle-changing surgeries, but we both came out clear of our cancers after about eight months of therapy. Thereafter, as we did our respective tests for the next two years, we eagerly exchanged notes and rejoiced as each of us came out clean. However, on the last test at the end of a two-year period, Gopalan was diagnosed with a new primary cancer. It was after this that we decided to write *Entrepreneurship Simplified*. Gopalan, with his experience of helping start-ups, was the primary author of the first three chapters of the book: 'Idea Generation and Validation', 'Funding Your Venture' and 'Winning with VCs'. Many potential entrepreneurs engaged in fundraising would tell me that they learnt so much from the chapter 'Funding Your Venture', which contained the distilled experience of Gopalan.

In this paperback version, I have added two new chapters, 'Strategic Sale of Your Company' and 'The Happiest Minds IPO Experience'. Gopalan would have been the primary author of both chapters had he not passed away.

Gopalan was happily with us when we launched *Entrepreneurship Simplified*. He participated and spoke at the launch event, though he was visibly unwell. A few days later, his son Siddharth got married, and Gopalan took part in all the festivities and functions. Chandra, his beloved wife, told me he was even more excited about the book launch than the wedding! Gopalan and I were already discussing our second book when he took a turn for the worse.

Chandra is an entrepreneur herself and an ultramarathon runner. When I told her of the paperback version, she said that hardly a day goes by without her thinking of Gopalan. I too have missed his sound advice as a board member and friend. These two additional chapters of *Entrepreneurship Simplified* are exclusively dedicated to Gopalan.

Ashok Soota

Preface

'If you cannot explain it simply, you don't understand it well enough'

—Albert Einstein

The objective of *Entrepreneurship Simplified* is to be a practical guide for you as an entrepreneur, with a view to improve the probability of success of your ventures. The book is addressed primarily to first-time entrepreneurs, including those still considering taking the entrepreneurial plunge. The thoughts and ideas given in *Entrepreneurship Simplified* are based on the experiences of the co-authors. We do believe that in a simple way we have been able to address the issues, challenges and dilemmas you will confront during your entrepreneurial journey, all the way from idea generation to your initial public offering (IPO). Daniel Isenberg (an ex-Harvard professor), in his book, *Worthless, Impossible and Stupid*, writes that, 'Entrepreneurship is hard. It is perceived as hard, it is experienced as hard, and it is objectively hard.' It is the aim of this book to show that while entrepreneurship *can* be hard, it need not always be so.

Entrepreneurship Simplified is a collaborative effort with S.R. Gopalan, my old friend, colleague, financial advisor and board member of Happiest Minds. Gopalan has founded a financial advisory organization, Dawn Consulting, which focuses on start-up ventures, and has worked with over fifty entrepreneurs, not including the many other entrepreneurial organizations for whom he has undertaken valuations. My own thoughts and suggestions in the book are based on several decades of intrapreneurial experience (at Shriram Refrigeration and Wipro) and my years with two entrepreneurial organizations—MindTree, where I was the founding chairman and managing director, and Happiest Minds, where I am the founding executive chairman. However, many takeaways contained in the book are owed even more to the incisive real-life questions raised by entrepreneurs at talks I have delivered on the subject and mentoring dialogues with many budding entrepreneurs.

Every chapter of *Entrepreneurship Simplified* is a collaborative effort between Gopalan and myself. However, Gopalan is the prime author of the chapters on funding, VCs and wealth creation, while I am the prime author for the rest of the chapters, except the last one on failure and success, which was jointly authored.

Since the book is intended to be a practical guide, as an entrepreneur it helps you in deciding:

- What and what not
- Why and why not
- How and how not
- When and when not

After examining all issues in the above context, we have summarized several practical takeaways at the end of each chapter and the top takeaways at the end of the book. How would we like you to use *Entrepreneurship Simplified* and derive the maximum benefits from it? In the first instance, we feel that an end-to-end reading is merited. Thereafter, you should revisit specific chapters with deep reflection when you are at the appropriate point in your entrepreneurial journey. For example, we have devoted almost the whole chapter on wealth creation and sharing to the Employee Stock Option Plan (ESOP). This is because it's your best way of rewarding your team, but it's an expensive scheme for your company and setting up an ESOP scheme is full of legal complexities. Ignoring these can lead to transferring to the taxman benefits which should be legitimately available to your team. Ideally, this is a chapter you should read and act upon a few months before you start your venture or, if your venture has already been launched, it should be absorbed at the earliest. Again, the chapter on the IPO should be revisited about two years before you embark on your public issue. Several other chapters like those on business strategy or marketing can, of course, be of benefit to you at every inflection point in your entrepreneurial journey.

We have placed three subjects in an appendix to the book as these may not be of interest to all: early- versus late-stage entrepreneurship, serial entrepreneurship and entrepreneurship in the same space as your previous employer. These will be of critical importance for some of you and the appended chapter does contain useful experiential anecdotes, including approaches to becoming a serial entrepreneur—a first-ever attempt to categorize serial entrepreneurs and identify the characteristics on which they build this capability.

While we believe that entrepreneurship need not be hard, we also do not want to create a sense of complacency that it can be a cakewalk. The entrepreneurial journey is full of challenges and does involve sacrifices, but we firmly believe that it should be a rewarding and joyous journey. We hope that *Entrepreneurship Simplified* will help you through this entire cycle from idea to IPO and beyond.

Bengaluru   Ashok Soota
1 June 2016

1.

Idea Generation and Validation

'Start-ups are only as good as where they end up'

—Alec Smart

'Where your start-up ends up is only as good as your idea'

—Ashok Soota

The starting point for a successful entrepreneurial venture is the right idea. How you generate potential ideas for your venture, how you choose the appropriate one and how you validate your selected idea to form the foundation for your venture's success or failure are key first steps. What you do later once you proceed, including building the organization, developing a business strategy and executing the idea, comprise the edifice built on the foundation of a validated idea. Somewhat surprisingly, in our mentoring conversations with potential and new entrepreneurs, we find that they seldom deliberate on their ideas and have hardly gone into sufficient depth to draw up and endorse a strategy before embarking on the venture.

But before we give you our thoughts on generating and validating ideas, a seeming digression.

The Verger

A verger, as some of you may know, is a church functionary. William Somerset Maugham, one of the most skilful exponents of the English language, in his story 'The Verger', creates an endearing protagonist, Albert Edward. Albert is an uneducated and illiterate person, and for fifteen years has been the proud and competent verger of St Peter's Church in the heart of London. One day, a new vicar arrives at the church who informs Albert that while he has no complaint against him, as a 'matter of prudence as well as of principle' he cannot retain an illiterate person as a verger.

But what, you may wonder, does this story have to do with idea generation and validation? Keeping the essence of the narrative intact, here follows a paraphrased and slightly modified version of what happens.

Albert takes the blow with seeming stoicism, but when he steps out on to the street he is in desperate need of a strong cup of tea. He sets down the street to look for a tea shop. Though it is a long street with all sorts of shops, he cannot find a single tea and pastry shop. He walks up and down the street again to make sure.

'I can't be the only man as walks along this street and wants a cup of tea,' he says. 'I shouldn't wonder but what a fellow might do very well with a little shop here. Tea and cakes, you know.' He is startled suddenly by his own thoughts.

'That's an idea,' he says. 'Strange 'ow things come to you when you least expect it.'

The very next day, Albert rents an empty shop on the street. Ten years later, he expands it to ten tea and pastry shops and builds himself a tidy fortune. The selection of each one of these locations was preceded by long walks on the street and around the neighbourhood to assess pedestrian traffic and ensure that there was no competition in the neighbourhood.

Albert had experienced the pain of an unfulfilled customer, which became the source of his idea. He validated it many times over by researching the neighbourhood, both from a supply and demand perspective. He also converted a problem into an opportunity—a very important entrepreneurial trait.

The Process of Choosing the Right Idea for Your Business

Now let's discuss what comes first: the entrepreneurial decision or the idea?

In the story 'The Verger', clearly the idea precedes Albert's decision to become an entrepreneur.

Sometimes the entrepreneurial opportunity seems so hot and so compelling that people who have never before considered becoming entrepreneurs decide to take the plunge. Such intuition was the driver during the dot-com days of the early noughties, when seasoned executives decided to quit their jobs and start IT services companies as Internet systems integrators or create dot-com entities. However, more often than not, a group of two to five friends from a common work or college background decide to become entrepreneurs and then start the search for an idea around which to build a business. Most teams we meet with have a single idea and quite quickly proceed to flesh out a business plan around the same. But we strongly believe that at least two or three ideas should be generated through brainstorming sessions, though only the most preferred one is to be taken through a validation process, which involves more than modest expenditure.

K. Ganesh is the most prolific serial entrepreneur in India, so much so that we could call him an 'Idea Factory'. He and his wife, Meena, are founder–promoters of four businesses which they have successfully sold—the last of which was TutorVista bought by Pearson. Most recently Ganesh, Meena and their partner, Srinivasan, have created a platform labelled the 'Growth Story'. Through this platform they generate and validate the idea and then seek a CEO who will lead the new company, despite which they remain closely involved in the running of the business. Under the Growth Story incubator, there are no less than thirteen companies—these include Big Basket, an online grocery delivery company and Portea, a home healthcare delivery service.

We asked Ganesh if he has a process for generating ideas, to which he responded that he:

- scans the market for 'big' customer pain points;
- chooses 'must have' rather than 'good to have' categories;
- thinks the idea must be scalable and therefore, command a decent market size;
- takes a five- to ten-year view on whether he can make a difference;
- thinks disproportionate value is created if he can be the first mover in an open field; and
- also thinks that though he likes to be early, it is important to not be too early in the market.

Peter Thiel, serial entrepreneur, the first outside investor in Facebook and author of *Zero to One*, was asked by the *Economic Times* how he would advise entrepreneurs searching for ideas. His first two responses are motherhood statements on which you can bear no disagreement—i.e. you should care strongly about the idea, and you should have good reason to think it will work. The third is puzzling: 'You should be the only one working on it.'

Logically, even if you are the first to start a new product/service category, any good idea will attract others to emulate it and/or to improve on it sooner than later. This tendency also reminds us of Daniel Isenberg's thesis in his book, *Worthless, Impossible and Stupid*, that entrepreneurs see what nobody else is able to, based on the premise that the 'hidden value' of an idea is perceived only by a chosen few. While this is largely correct, we think there's nothing to prevent others from becoming fast followers.

However, we do feel that both these statements set the bar too high for new ideas. Everyone can't be a Steve Jobs or an Elon Musk. You don't have to be a super genius to get a great entrepreneurial idea and you don't need to be the one and only player in a given space.

So how do you select the right idea for your venture?

First, start backwards from what you want to be in terms of size and scale. David Thomson in his book, *Blueprint to a Billion*, says that the probability of an idea being converted into a billion-dollar business is one in 20,000. We live today in the age of unicorns, or private companies with a valuation of $1 billion or more, with the global number of unicorn companies around 150 and growing. While half of these are in the US, the rate of growth is actually highest in China and India, which are home to the second and third largest number of unicorns.

Now it can be tempting to aim to be a unicorn, but to this we would like to suggest a principle: Your idea should be commensurate with your ambition, and your ambition must be based on a realistic assessment of your capability and your core competence. For example, Ashok sees his core competence as building and rapidly scaling organizations. Accordingly, it would not make sense for him to choose a business that does not have a large market size and opportunity.

It is also nice to describe one's idea as disruptive, but this is also a much misused word. Disruptive technologies alone do not make for a disruptive business. For something to truly merit being called disruptive, it would need to create a new business model or new ways of reaching customers or a new ways of delivering a service. Disruptive businesses would potentially reduce the cost of doing business by an order of magnitude.

Ashok suggests the following approaches for generating new business ideas:

- Use a 'kaleidoscope' approach, where a small turn throws open a whole new configuration. A small change, be it in a product or service or business model, can throw open a new entrepreneurial opportunity. Fairly common in this regard are business-to-business (B2B) models where the new entrant converted the model into business-to-business-to-consumer (B2B2C); lesser known are examples of the converse: in essence business-to-consumer (B2C) models, but where the revenue model is on a B2B basis. A good example of the latter is OneAssist, one of the earliest customers of Happiest Minds. Though the services of OneAssist are clearly directed to the individual customer, the process of customer acquisition is B2B. The car rental businesses of Uber and Ola can also be considered applications of the kaleidoscope model. Before they were created, people already had access to car-hire services, but new technologies were used to create a new model for bringing customers and suppliers together.

  To explore the 'kaleidoscope' approach, you can ask yourself the following questions with respect to an existing service:

  o Can we change the asset ownership structure?
  o Can we reduce the idle time of assets deployed in the business?

o   Can we introduce pay for use?

o   Can we 'platformize' the business for greater flexibility?

o   Can some participants in the current model be transformed from employees to entrepreneurs, such as the case of drivers at Uber?

o   Can we convert some costs from fixed to variable?

o   What parts of service delivery can be automated?

o   How do we improve the customer experience?

Each of these questions is like the turn of a kaleidoscope, which can throw up a new business model.

- Look at failed dot-coms. Many of them had the plug pulled too early when the dot-com bust came. Also, there is a scope to reinvent many of them as Web 3.0 or Web 4.0/5.0 ventures. Thus you see the revival of a failed Shaadi.com in a new form and, in the same sector, a Bharat Matrimony.com.

- Look at globally successful ideas and 'localize' them. While it is true that many ideas emanate from the US, it would be a disaster to just copy these point blank. Also, cross-border flow of ideas is not a one-way street. Considering the huge Indian and Chinese diaspora spread across the world, many businesses catering to their needs can be introduced elsewhere and adopted by wider communities. Interestingly, some of the most exciting new applications in the mobile world are first being developed and launched in developing countries as they can straightaway leapfrog to the latest technologies and business models.

7

Change is the Opportunity

Our firm view is that change is the source of most new opportunities, be it social change, generational aspirations or technological change. Also, since the speed and spread of change keeps increasing, the good news is that opportunities are limitless. Much of change is driven by technological advances which make possible new ways of reaching customers, new business models, new ways of delivering a service, etc. Accordingly, it's important to track the major technology changes and leverage their power for new businesses or include them into your products or services.

For example, though both MindTree and Happiest Minds were IT services companies, they leveraged technology changes which fuelled a demand explosion. When Ashok and his co-founders launched MindTree in August 1999, the Internet explosion had nurtured the dot-com boom. This enabled them to enter the market as e-System integrators, which further allowed them to position MindTree as competing not with the Indian IT services companies but the US e-System integrators like Scient, Viant, Lante and a dozen other similar entities. This also enabled MindTree to get US company minus prices (instead of Indian company pricing) with the added benefit of lower costs of executing delivery from India. Consequently, within six months, MindTree was able to break even. What followed when the dot-com bust happened is another story, but suffice it to say that MindTree was almost the sole survivor—going on to do a successful IPO—out of about 100 such e-System integrators globally that sprang up around that time.

In the decade following the Internet bust, many new disruptive technologies came up such as social media, mobility, analytics and cloud (popularly known collectively as SMAC). These technology developments were soon followed by unified communications, big data, Internet of things (IoT), and artificial intelligence/cognitive computing. These advances enabled companies, particularly new start-ups, to deliver their products as a service, to develop omnichannel capability and reduce their infrastructure costs significantly. For Happiest Minds, the narrative was always about SMACPLUS solutions.

Though the Internet spawned some 100 new IT services companies, in spite of all the noted technology changes, no new Indian IT services came up to focus only on integrating all the new technologies to create digital transformation solutions. This enabled Happiest Minds to occupy this vacant slot to position itself as a focused digital transformation services provider, probably the only of its kind which derived almost all its revenue from transformation services, such as improving customer experience, delivering a product as a service or providing agile infrastructure for digital environments.

Apart from the SMACPLUS technologies, the Internet too has been evolving, all the way from Web 1.0 in the dot-com days to Web 5.0 now.

The first implementation of the World Wide Web, invented by Tim Berners Lee, was essentially a read-only web. Web 1.0 was a static publishing and transaction medium. It was the web of the dot-com boom, but also bred companies like Google, Yahoo, Rediffusion etc. It also enabled e-commerce and led to the birth of Amazon and the many e-tailers that followed suit.

Web 2.0 was the participating and co-created web. Content could now be created collaboratively and published for global audiences. Companies which came up in the era of Web 2.0 included Twitter, YouTube, Facebook and Wikipedia. Globally, many media aggregation companies also owed their success to Web 2.0.

Web 3.0, popularly known as the semantic and intelligent web, enabled communication between users and applications, leading to sharing and collaboration among users and the creation of many web services. According to Nova Spivack, 'Web 3.0 is a set of standards that turns the web into one big database.' Web 3.0 has implications for design, creation of 3D portals and improved search functions, to mention just a few of its applications.

Web 4.0 is a further extension of Web 3.0, connecting the web to its mobile surroundings and enabling the connection to the web from all devices in the real and virtual world in real time. You can visualize the thousands of new businesses the mobile web has made possible, including 3D holographs and medical applications whereby the disabled can control a computer through their thoughts.

Finally, Web 5.0, which is still evolving, is the open, linked and emotional web. Today, potential entrepreneurs are combining technologies like SMAC, big data, IoT, artificial intelligence/cognitive computing with sentiment analysis to create new businesses based on Web 5.0. In these applications, feelings and emotions are captured for decision-making, including for e-commerce applications.

An important clarification: The development of newer generations of the web does not make the older web versions obsolete. For your business idea, you should use whichever web version is suitable for your needs and for delivering your business proposition.

Leveraging newer technologies is critical for companies entering a highly competitive field. Arista Networks, led by Jayshree Ullal, an Ernst & Young 'Entrepreneur of the Year', has done this very successfully to compete against the likes of Cisco and Juniper. Arista offers a software-defined cloud networking platform with Web 5.0 capability to meet the needs of hyper-scale computing environments with ultra-low latency needs.

The other good news is that it's never been easier to start and build a company and take it global. Many companies now need minimal brick-and-mortar infrastructure as they are increasingly becoming virtual companies operating in cyberspace.

Such changes open up innumerable opportunities in virtually every industry as change is everywhere, be it biotech, alternate energy, retail, media, healthcare and so on. Even driverless cars would not have been possible without the new SMACPLUS technologies. Take a sector like healthcare in particular. We already have multiple differentiated entrants covering areas like health monitoring devices, residential healthcare delivery services, second opinion.com, etc. We are personally in touch with two other healthcare portals currently in stealth mode. The e-commerce wave is currently being followed by a hyperlocal wave. Nano technologies, virtual reality, 3D-printing and wearables are amongst many other new technologies creating new business opportunities. In effect, the opportunities due to change are limitless.

Due to these technology-driven changes, there is an opportunity for disintermediation in virtually every industry that can enable disruptive business models: disruptive for incumbents and opportunities for new entrants.

What Is the Importance of Being a First Mover?

How important is it to be the first mover in a new space? There is undoubtedly some advantage to be the first off the block in virgin territory. Entrepreneurs like Elon Musk or K. Ganesh swear by this approach.

However, it should be remembered that being the first mover often requires investments in creating a market and proving a concept. As a first mover you have to take higher risks. Even while the concept is being proven, you have to scale rapidly to ensure market leadership before someone comes along with the promise of a better, cheaper, faster solution, service or product. Microsoft did not develop the first operating system, Google was not the first search engine, Facebook was not the first social media platform and the Apple iPad was not the first product in its genre.

Whether you are the first mover, a fast follower or even a late entrant in a market, you should aim to be in the top three in your space and remain unafraid of competition. The highest valued companies often operate in the most competitive spaces. The top player in an industry will typically have a higher market capitalization than the next four or five companies combined. The top two will almost certainly have a higher market cap than the rest of the top ten combined. This is quite evident for companies like Google or Apple. It's equally so for Toyota, whose market valuation for many years has exceeded that of the top three US automakers combined (General Motors, Ford, Chrysler). Even in a $150 billion industry like Indian IT, while the industry was growing very rapidly, all major players rode the wave and were not too far apart in terms of market valuation. As the market slowed, Tata Consultancy Services (TCS), the number one player in size, surged ahead, overtook Infosys as the number one market valuation company and then went on to exceed for some time the combined valuations of Infosys, Wipro, HCL and Tech Mahindra.

A first-mover advantage does not guarantee market leadership. So in aiming for leadership, you should also define your market very specifically. For example, Happiest Minds, operating in a large market and being a very late entrant, could never hope to be one of the top five Indian IT services players. But if we define our space as digital transformation, we can certainly look at being a top five player, first in customer mindshare and in course of time revenues as well. We can also look at specific segments like security and edutech, where there are large paradigm shifts and being a late entrant actually facilitates provision of the latest solutions.

There is a caveat though, regarding the desire to be only in the top three or five. In a large industry, even being in the top ten can create large value. For example, MindTree may have been the 150th entrant into the Indian IT industry, but today it is ranked tenth by revenue, with a market cap exceeding US$ 1.5 billion.

Idea Validation

As an introduction to this module, we would like to describe how Alok Mittal, entrepreneur-turned-VC-turned-entrepreneur (JobsAhead to Canaan Partners to Indifi) went about generating and validating his idea for his second venture, Indifi. In his first venture, Alok was clear that he would do something by leveraging the Internet and, without looking at many options, created JobsAhead. After the dot-com bust, he was able to have it successfully acquired by Monster.com.

This time around, he wanted to give himself enough choices before he finalized one idea for his new venture. He first perused a list of the 5000 fastest growing companies in the US. From this, he culled out six or seven ideas which, with suitable adaptation, could apply to India. After further scrutiny, he reduced the selected potential ideas to three in very different industries/ spaces: one was an offline tutoring model in the education space, the second was a consumer-centric health offering and the third, a cloud-lending platform for small businesses. Though Alok had an overall understanding of each of these spaces, he did not have deep domain knowledge in any of them. Accordingly, he socialized the ideas for feedback within his own LinkedIn and Facebook networks, not just to validate them, but also to seek interest from potential co-founders. He felt that the choice of co-founders would depend on the industry he would select, to bring in the depth of knowledge he lacked. For all three ideas he decided to do some low-cost information gathering; for example, for the education venture, he engaged an agency to do a quantitative study with 400 potential customers.

All three ideas were studied in parallel and eventually the healthcare and education ideas were dropped. Apart from Alok's personal meetings with potential lenders and borrowers, what swung the decision towards the cloud-lending platform was the ability to tie in an Anchor Partner, a travel-ticketing consolidator who was in a position to help originate the business through an existing network of 7000 travel agents. Unlike the first time round, Alok took the idea early to VCs. Finding investor demand to be greater than his need for equity was itself a great validator. Interestingly, he chose two institutional investors, and though they could have put in all the equity that was needed, he personally invested and also brought in five individual investors who he felt could provide useful insights for the business, i.e. 'intelligent money'.

The entire process from starting to selecting the idea to finalizing funding took Alok eight months.

Let us see some of the principles we can derive on 'idea validation' from Alok's approach and experience. First, we will notice that he socialized the idea with a wide variety of persons from both his social and professional network. This is very colourfully described by Debra Amidon in her visual story book, *In Search of Innovation*. The booklet is a story of how an idea is transformed into an economically viable innovation. First, she shares the idea with every friend she knows and few others she doesn't know. Some say it's very good, some laugh at it and say it's crazy, some say they wished they had thought up the idea themselves, some say they can't understand it at all while some even try to steal it. All through this journey of ups and downs, the idea is modified, adapted and enriched till it's ready for taking to the world.

Another aspect which comes through in Amidon's book and in Alok's story is the importance of the idea, developing your own comfort and strengthening your conviction in it. For the entire gestation period you must live, breathe, dream the idea. You should visualize how it will grow from a seed to a tree.

Another aspect of idea validation that can be learned from Alok's story is that he took his idea to VCs and individual investors. The positive response from several of them for sums greater than his needs was a reassuring validation as external investors have 'been there, done that' many times over. Alok also received many suggestions from the investors which helped him reshape the idea.

One other approach to idea validation is a more structured and formal one: of testing the same. Determining feasibility may be through market research, focus groups and/or a pilot launch. There can be occasions when the founders know the industry/market well and time to market is crucial. In such cases, upfront, big bang commitments to the venture are merited and the pilot phase can be omitted, as it was in the case of Happiest Minds.

For B2C businesses, Jessie Paul of Paul Writer has mentioned to Ashok a simple ABCD model that she heard from David E. Bell of Harvard University at a seminar:

A—Added value: What this offering does over existing offerings in the market
B—Behavioural change required to use it: This should be minimal.
C—Complexity: How hard is it to figure out?
D—Diffusion: Can the product sell itself? Will others know you are using it?

There are several other questions which you, the entrepreneur, have to ask yourself regarding validation. First, is the idea scalable? To determine scalability, it's important to get a good understanding of the market size. Quite often, total market data is available through secondary sources. However, this can be very misleading. What is needed is an accurate assessment of the addressable market for your venture. This may require market segmentation in multiple ways, by classifying customers and seeing which proportion have a need for your offering. For example, Portea.com, the home physiotherapy service by Meena Ganesh and K. Ganesh, was conceived after Meena's father came out of hospital, and they found that post-procedural services delivered to residences were not available. Portea obviously addressed a customer pain point; many ideas are generated and validated by responding to pain points in such a manner. However, in sizing the market, it would be essential to assess which proportion of the population would be willing to pay premiums for such convenience. Also, which types of injuries would be more amenable for persons wanting home care? For example, those injuries impacting a person's mobility, such as a foot or knee injury, would have a high share of the addressable market, but this may not be the case for arm or shoulder injuries.

Similarly, for Happiest Minds, if we defined our market size as the entire India outsourcing market, we would believe we are operating in a market of about US$150 billion. However, since we planned to focus only on disruptive technologies and digital transformation, we needed to reconsider the market by backing out the many segments in which we wouldn't operate. Likewise, no customer is going to give a $25 million project to a service provider which is sub $100 million to avoid overdependence on the one customer and also because of a perceived risk for the customer. We were effectively shut out from such large businesses until we became a much larger company—which we needed to factor in as well as we sized our addressable market.

For idea validation, it's also important to look at existing and future competition, which has a nasty way of emerging from unexpected sources and directions. Also be prepared, that if you are very successful, larger companies with much deeper pockets will want to invade your space. Will your venture be defensible against such attacks? A corollary to this is: do you see yourself as having the ability to introduce a stream of differentiators? Remember that all differentiators have a shelf-life and therefore, you need to continuously differentiate to ensure the defensibility of your idea.

Plan ahead. Visualize the ways in which your business can fail and be clear about how you will develop plans to overcome the hurdles and also have the wherewithal, both mental and financial, to see through the challenges. This exercise should include noting a few well-articulated risks and not the laundry list of all possible risks in an IPO filing statement or the warnings which accompany most prescription medicines! The capital intensity of the business becomes important here, particularly the danger of your industry moving out of the preferred investment category for investors—because most industries witness such boom cycles followed by cycles when fundraising becomes difficult.

Additionally, an important validation question for your venture is whether the timing is right. If yours is a new product or service, is the market ready for it? Does the required ecosystem/infrastructure exist to support its success? A good example of the importance of timing is the failure of FabMart in Bangalore in the early years of this century and the success of Big Basket in recent years. In the period 2000–04, smartphones and other multichannel access points for ordering didn't exist, and Bangalore didn't have an adequate broadband infrastructure. Consequently, FabMart, which was otherwise a well-managed start-up with a robust platform, couldn't build the critical mass. It was ahead of its time!

When you have put your idea through a validation wringer and looked at it with realistic optimism, it should pass what Ashok calls the 'head, heart and gut' test. The head gives you the cerebral underpinning, the many things discussed in this chapter, the pros and cons, all backed by numbers wherever possible. The heart speaks to your emotions. Is the idea one which you are enthused about? Will it help you create an organization which will bring joy and happiness to the team? Finally, the gut is your instinct or intuition on how the venture will work out in a five-year-plus time frame. Do you feel that five years from now, you will look back with satisfaction at the choice you made? If you find your head, heart and gut aligned, go ahead and press the 'go' button. Odds are you have a winning proposition. But if your head, heart and gut are not fully aligned, step back to the drawing board and tweak your idea or your business, or consult a mentor. Even then some doubts may remain. Entrepreneurship is all about risk-taking and if you see the risks as being manageable—go ahead and take the plunge.

KEY TAKEAWAYS

✓ The single most important decision you will make in your entrepreneurial venture is the choice of your idea around which you will build your business.
✓ Your chosen idea must solve a customer pain or be a new way of delivering an existing service or disrupt existing businesses.

✓ Change creates opportunities. Much of the change is driven by new technologies which make new business models possible or create new services. It is important to understand the business creating power of such technologies. Also, as the pace of change keeps increasing, opportunities are limitless.

✓ Don't just zero in on an idea when starting a business. Give yourself a choice of two or three. Use the 'kaleidoscope' approach to generate new ideas. Also look at new technology developments such as Web 3.0 to Web 5.0, SMAC, big data, artificial intelligence (AI), Internet of things (IoT), etc. to see what new businesses and new business models they are enabling.

✓ Before zeroing in on your chosen idea, do some low-cost information gathering and validation of your preferred idea. Socialize your idea widely and live, breathe, dream it till you are ready to make a choice.

✓ It is preferable to be the first mover in an industry, but essential to be an early and differentiated entrant. It's important to have the goal of being amongst the top three players in your chosen space.

✓ For validation, put your idea through the scalability and defensibility tests.

✓ Remember that all differentiators have a shelf-life and a stream of differentiators will be needed to ensure defensibility.

✓ Examine if the timing is right. Is the market ready for it? Some ventures fail because they are too early for the market.

✓ Take your final decision using the 'head, heart and gut' principle.

2.

Funding Your Venture

'An entrepreneur without funding is a musician without an instrument'

—Robert A. Rice Jr

The area on which we get the most questions from new or potential entrepreneurs is invariably related to funding the venture. The ambit of questions includes the desirability of bootstrapping, angel investing versus venture capitalist (VC) investments, the right amount to raise, and approaching new investors like private equity (PE) players for subsequent rounds. The final stage for fundraising is the IPO, but since our conversations are mostly with potential or early-stage entrepreneurs, the IPO seldom arises for discussion. However, we do advise that entrepreneurs should have an approximate understanding on the time to IPO as this will determine the exit strategy for investors. If the thought process is to avoid an IPO and seek a strategic investor to monetize the wealth created, entrepreneurs should also be clear whether this is an option or a Plan B. In his two entrepreneurial experiences (MindTree and Happiest Minds), Ashok was always clear that he was building businesses which he would take public. This was clearly communicated to the investors (VCs in both cases) upfront and the period indicated as six or seven years, so that the right expectations were set from the word go.

Bootstrapping: Merits and Demerits

The one big argument for bootstrapping (a situation in which an entrepreneur builds a company with personal capital, generally a small amount), even if external investors are available, is when deferring the induction of investors might ensure a significantly higher valuation. However, as we will show later in this chapter, there are multiple approaches to increasing valuation. In essence, we are mostly in favour of seeking external investors from the start.

The reasons for this approach are multiple. Firstly, good investors not only validate your idea but also help you to modify and adapt it. They also add value in multiple ways, such as adapting your business model, sharing your risk, identifying talent, introducing you to their partner ecosystem and so on.

To be fair, there are many bootstrapped ventures that have grown to become profitable as mentioned in an article titled 'Living Bootstrapped' (*Economic Times*, 17 January 2016). These examples include SignEasy, Zoho and Fusioncharts. While the founders in these cases seem happy with their decision to bootstrap, the issue is how much larger or more valuable the company could have become with external funding.

If the founders do have funds to invest in the venture, we see it as preferable to put these in as part of the first round. The external investors will see it as a positive that the founders are putting their own neck on the line. Also, the founders' money comes in on equal terms with the investors' money with respect to valuation. In a sense you become your own VC with such an approach.

On the other hand, if the founders put in all their investible funds into bootstrapping, there is a big danger that they will run short of cash by the time they are negotiating with VCs. There is nothing worse than handling such negotiations with your back to the wall. The prospect of dwindling cash and unpaid salaries creates anxieties and may lead to accepting the very first offer which comes the founders' way. You will come across entrepreneurs who took the bootstrapping path and are happy with the results. More often, though, it's an invitation to years of skimping and personal sacrifice while you watch others sail by you in scale and profitability.

Also, once in the market, ventures should be ramped up quickly to avoid others getting into the game. Adequate money is one of the fuels for such acceleration. A combination of investor funds and founder funds increases the pool size.

Finally, the main reason we are against bootstrapping is that we've seen too many founders blow up their life savings trying to get a venture off the ground and then failing.

Angels or VCs?

Odds are that there will be as many views on whether to seek angel or VC funding as there are entrepreneurs. Prajakt Raut, entrepreneur and entrepreneurship evangelist, sees many advantages (and some disadvantages) in starting with angel investors over VCs. Ashok's view is somewhat different. Angel investors will typically invest only up to $1 million in your venture and the way cash gets burned while creating a business, you will soon be knocking on the door of VCs anyway. In a majority of cases, the bulk of the organization's pre-IPO life will be spent with them as your investors. Since every round involves some dilution, you may as well go straight to the VCs if you can get them interested in your venture. Prajakt's view is that VCs and angel investors give different kinds of advice and that angel investors would be more likely to help you with the 'fundamentals of the business at the starting point and guide you through the setting-up stage'. Our view is that a good VC will provide valuable assistance at this stage as well.

An excellent article by Karthika Krishnamurthy titled 'Power of Ideas: How Angel Investment Networks Are Pushed to Innovate in a Changing Market' (*Economic Times*, 9 October 2015) gives a comprehensive understanding of the available angel networking opportunities (mostly in India, but with some global references too). In the article, Mohan Kumar of Norwest Venture Partners comments that the 'deal flow from traditional angel networks has dropped in the past few years. We rarely hear from them anymore. Instead, accelerators and incubators have started reaching out'. We have however noted that the Angel ecosystem has of late been very active and hence should not be underestimated. Kris Gopalakrishnan, Infosys co-founder and a member of the Indian Angel Network, says that 'at the end of the day, I see all these networks as complementary. All kinds of models can coexist today because there is a need of early-stage capital'. Since 2015, the entrepreneurial boom has also seen increased activity in the angel investing space. Investors like Sharad Sharma, Mohandas Pai, Rajan Anandan and many others are contributing to creating hundreds of start-ups every year. An article titled 'Mumbai's Home to the Highest Number of Angel Investors' (*Times of India*, 25 May 2016) says that in 2015, the number of angel deals almost doubled to 691.

The good news for entrepreneurs is that there is a wide choice of angel investors and VCs available. And the choice is not limited to angels and VCs; today, we have a wide variety of options available, including online dealmaking platforms and crowdsourcing for funds. A comprehensive article on crowdfunding by Venkatesh Babu in *Business Today* lists the major crowdfunding platforms as LetsVenture, termsheet. io, Investopad and Catapooolt. Many of the crowdsourcing platforms have a preference for social sector projects. These include Ketto, Fueladream and BitGiving. The indicative amounts raised by crowdsourced projects are similar or somewhat higher than those available from angel investors.

If you are seeking entities which can provide funds of say $3 million or more, like VCs, the alternatives are large companies which are now making strategic investments in start-ups. These include Alibaba from China and the large IT companies like Infosys and Wipro. Investors for even bigger ticket spends of $25 million and more are the PE players like KKR, Apollo, Carlyle and the sovereign funds of the Middle East countries.

Since we feel that the single largest vehicle for early-stage investment is VC firms, our next chapter will focus on negotiating with and 'living' with VCs—many of the points will also be applicable to handling other categories of investors.

What Is the Right Amount of Money to Be Raised?

The single most often asked question we get from founders is: 'How much money should I raise?' We'd like to define a few principles to answer this:

- First, assess the total money you will need before the company reaches cash break even.
- Add to this a sum for acquisitions to be made if these are likely to be part of your strategy.

- The total number you'll yield from the steps above determines the amount of money you are required to raise till the IPO or whatever exit you plan to make.
- Decide whether you want to raise this amount in two, three or four rounds. Since each round will involve its own dilution, two or three rounds should be preferred as the maximum, though we are aware that many product companies in the US opt for as many as five rounds. Another example for multiple investment rounds is the e-commerce players who have an enormous appetite for funds and are able to raise these at ever-increasing valuations.
- At no time should the venture be left with less than six months' cash to fund operations. Accordingly, the first round (plus founders' funds, if any) should be adequate for a minimum of two years. Our preference would be three years.
- Allow six-plus months for negotiations for each round. Legal agreements can take a long time to consummate and it is necessary to be patient. Entrepreneurs have to plan for this. Accordingly, discussions for the 'next' round should begin when you still have at least twelve months of cash.

While the single largest reason for ventures to fold up is the non-availability of funds, we should also caution against raising too much money. One danger is, obviously, more dilution than necessary. Another is that with an excess of funds, it's difficult to bring about a culture of doing 'more with less' and implement cost control. We did experience these repercussions at Happiest Minds where our first fundraising round was worth $52.5 million. The founder dilution aspect was neutralized by Ashok investing a significant part of the above himself.

Maximizing Valuation

When we talk of maximizing valuation, we should emphasize that this is not just a first round exercise, but a strategy needed for every round.

In the first round, the key determinants of valuation are the 'idea', the 'team', and the 'business plan', comprising the strategic/marketing/financial plans. The issues around idea validation have been addressed in detail in the first chapter. From our experience, most entrepreneurs are weakest on the strategic and marketing plans. This may just be because many of them are 'techies' excited about the technological coolness of their product and idea. With entrepreneurs getting younger by the day, most have limited understanding of the dynamics of sales and marketing. We have covered this aspect extensively in our chapter on marketing.

The area which is always complete but most suspect is the financial plan. Every budding entrepreneur has no difficulty in finding an accountant to prepare the predictably increasing revenue charts with attractive profitability within a short time frame. We would seriously caution entrepreneurs to refrain from making overly optimistic projections. Firstly, any experienced VC will see through this immediately and appropriately discount the projections. They will also likely make the assumption that there is a high probability of one of several low-probability external events occurring to create setbacks. If you have confidence in your idea and your team, you don't have to overstate your numbers. If you do so, these can come back and bite you. The VC may include these as a condition to be met and a revaluation to occur if these numbers are not achieved, or some other clause which increases investor per cent holding. An example is given in the next chapter.

Once the business plan is accepted by the investors, the projections for year five can be a good basis for arriving at the likely values that same year. This can be discounted to arrive at the current valuation.

Determining the right value for a start-up is never easy. But if there have been past buy/sell transactions in that space, the revenue or profit multiples in such transactions would be a good indicator to develop an idea of what the valuation can be. However, in the end, the agreed valuation number for settling on equity to investors will be a negotiated number.

A very important influencer on valuation is timing. The investing community goes through cycles of over-optimism and realistic reassessment followed by pessimism. Also, certain industries are 'flavours of the day'. From the entrepreneur's angle, it's best to catch one of these upward waves. For example, at MindTree we did our first round at the height of the dot-com boom. Six months later, we would not have received even half the valuation we received (and therefore, double the dilution), and nine months later, we wouldn't have even been able to raise any money based on our positioning as an Internet system integrator.

Cash to Next Round Decision-making

Strategies for conserving your cash are the best way to optimize use of your funds and therefore, we feel it's appropriate to include this section here.

We suggest that the founding CEO (and CFO) institute a 'cash to next round' principle for their decision-making. To illustrate this through an example, Ashok says:

When my co-founders at MindTree reached out to me (though old colleagues, we had discovered each other through a VC firm, Walden), they had been in discussion for several months to raise $5 million of cash. They had also prepared a business plan, where a significant amount of this money would have gone into buying land and building a development centre. On a P & L calculation basis, seen in a seven-year cycle, this could have been the superior alternative to renting a facility. Although I had already got a commitment for $10 million, I was able to convince them that on a cash flow basis, this would significantly reduce our time to the next round. Assuming we raised our market valuation by at least 50 per cent in this interim period, we could raise the same amount of money next time with a much lower level of dilution. In this particular case, it not only allowed us to defer our next round, it ensured the survival of MindTree. An Internet systems integrator starting with $5 million of cash, half of it buried in land/buildings, would have been amongst the first few to collapse when the dot-com bust arrived.

Another expenditure that is very high on the cash wastefulness index is 'too soon' acquisitions. We were very surprised by the number of early-stage companies in the dot-com boom days which made acquisitions of similar start-ups at a huge premium only for the combined entity to fold up a few months later. The only ones to gain were the shareholders who sold out. More recently, we had Flipkart acquiring another e-commerce start-up, Myntra. Though Flipkart was flush with funds after its successive fundraising rounds at high valuations, it might soon face challenges requiring all its ammunition in view of Amazon's recent successful entry into India. Another example is Zomato, which made a highly publicized acquisition of NextTable in the US, only to be forced to lay off several hundred persons a few months later to keep their operations afloat.

To be fair, not just start-ups make such mistakes. Globally, it will be difficult to find an example as dramatic as Kingfisher Airlines and its acquisition of the cash-deficit Deccan Aviation. The latter had pioneered low-cost flying in India, but its balance sheet was a mess and subsequent funding was not coming through. Kingfisher Airlines had established a reputation as the best full-service carrier in India and a great brand in a short time, but was also losing money. First, through its ill-conceived acquisition, Kingfisher killed Deccan's market as they just didn't know how to run a low-cost airline. Kingfisher, in the meanwhile, had grandiose plans of introducing the first non-stop Bangalore–San Francisco flight. Even while all these plans were being aired, suddenly one day, Kingfisher announced the cancellation of scores of flights without any warning. They didn't have enough money to keep the entire fleet flying! Apparently, they didn't see this crisis coming until it was too late. The market reacted with horror and it began the unravelling and quick demise of what could have been India's finest airline. (Technically, the company still exists but without any operations.)

Availability and Ease of Securing Funding

There has never been a better time to become an entrepreneur than now. The current global explosion in entrepreneurship, though driven by innovation, has been fuelled by the vast amount of venture capital available.

For several decades now and for many more ahead, the hotspot with the maximum available venture funding has been Palo Alto in Silicon Valley, California. There are more VCs per mile on Sand Hill Road in Palo Alto than any other place in the world. We are making a correlation here between the number of VCs and the amount of capital, and the ease of raising funds; this could be erroneous, because the investors there are seasoned and very discerning. But the real good news is that this large pool of capital is accessible from many parts of the world. With an increasing number of companies seeking to become global, the same VCs can be approached for investment whether you are an entrepreneur in the UK, China, Australia, India or elsewhere. The investments can come from the VCs' global funds or, depending on the VC, from country-specific funds. When we presented the Happiest Minds investment case to Canaan, the virtual meeting had attendees from Canaan partners located in Tel Aviv, Boston, Silicon Valley and India.

In each of the major growth economies, local venture funds have also come up strong, along with many other international sources. SoftBank in Japan is a fund that is very active globally. Many UK, Singapore and Middle East funds have also operated in India for many years.

We believe that India is probably one of the easiest markets to raise funds in the world at present and there is definitely more money available chasing good ideas than the other way around. The valuation and excitement levels have increased because India has also created a few unicorns, not to mention Flipkart which, within a few years, has skyrocketed to the valuation of $15 billion. There are seven unicorns in India today and there is every likelihood that five years from now there will be fifteen to twenty, or more.

We have recently met with delegations of young entrepreneurs from Canada and Europe. One of the most frequent questions put forth by them is, not surprisingly, regarding funding. Ashok advises them to create an India connection for their venture and raise the money in India.

Now apart from geographic considerations, what are the other factors which can contribute to the ease of raising funds, and that too, at a good valuation? First, as we identified in the previous section, is the nature of the idea and whether it fits into the 'genres of ideas' which are currently preferred investments for the VCs. You could call this a 'follow the money' approach.

The track record of the founder or founders can also make a huge difference. That said, we are not necessarily making a case for late-stage entrepreneurship. Still, Ashok's experience is worth narrating. He is fond of saying that in the MindTree start-up days, when he was fifty-eight-years-old, he raised the money through a phone call to the US. Within an hour of leaving Azim Premji's office (where he agreed on a six-month transition to enable Wipro to get a new CEO on board), he was on the phone with Walden in the US and had a commitment for $10 million. Ashok also specified the percentage he'd like to part with (he eventually settled at $9.5 million for the valuation he asked on the call). While this is true, it's also fair to state that the MindTree first round VCs (Walden of US and GTV of India) had been in touch with Ashok months earlier, suggesting he start off on his own. The 'hot space' factor also played a role as all this happened at the height of the dot-com boom.

Eleven years later, when Ashok started Happiest Minds and IT services were no longer a preferred space for investors, things were not as easy. Here his track record helped even more. Within four months of starting discussions the investor money was in the bank. What really helped in this case was Ashok's keenness to invest a significant amount himself. In both cases, being able to project a strong founding team also helped.

Even more compelling and powerful is the example of Dave Duffield. At the age of sixty-five, shortly after the acquisition of PeopleSoft (a company he co-founded), he left and was able to raise vast sums for starting Workday, a cloud-based, Software as a Service (SaaS) delivery model competitor to his prior company. Clearly, in this case, his track record helped enormously.

Having mentioned a benefit of late-stage entrepreneurship, it's only fair to add that the average age of entrepreneurs is reducing the world over and young entrepreneurs are raising vast amounts of money at very good valuations. The average work experience of an entrepreneur in India today is estimated as seven years—and dropping. We don't think there is any 'right age' to become an entrepreneur. You are ready when you are ready and that's the right time and age to take the plunge.

Exploring Debt and Other Sources of Raising Funds

It is desirable to explore funding options other than equity. The Government of India's MSME Guarantee Scheme provides an opportunity to get up to Rs 1 crore funding from banks without any security. In case of companies operating in high-tech areas, funding from the government's technology development fund is a very viable option. This comes primarily in the form of a loan with a small portion of the loan that is convertible into equity.

Some of the state government venture capital funds offer funding by way of a mix of debt and equity. The equity taken is generally a nominal amount, less than 20 per cent, whereas the bulk of the amount is given by way of a loan. So long as the company is able to service the loan, this is also a very good option.

Another way to reduce the initial fund requirement is to consider incubation centres which are now available across the country, in many universities as well as in non-university locations.

Overall, we do feel it's generally not a good idea to take debt on to your balance sheet until you have cash flows to support the servicing of the debt. After this debt serviceability is reached, moderate debt is a preferred option if equity raising can be delayed with a view to getting a much higher valuation and consequently, lower dilution in the next round.

KEY TAKEAWAYS

✓ If the company is able to get an attractive valuation upfront, it is better to get external investment rather than bootstrap. External funding provides the fuel to accelerate to market, apart from the assistance provided by VCs. Also, too many founders blow up their life savings while trying to bootstrap.

✓ Founders' investments, if any, can be done along with the first round so that money from internal and external sources comes in at the same valuation. In a sense, you become your own VC.

✓ Angel investors will seldom invest more than $1 million. If this means you will very quickly be knocking on VCs' doors, it is best to go to them straightaway.

✓ The most important factor for funding is your assessment of the cash required to break even. This becomes the minimum amount to be raised across one or more rounds. Add to this the money needed for acquisitions, if any.

✓ Once you've arrived at the break-even number, then work out a strategy to raise this amount with minimum dilution.

✓ The first round should preferably be adequate for two years or more. Negotiations for any subsequent round should begin when you are down to cash levels adequate for twelve months.

✓ There has to be a strategy for each round.

- ✓ The valuation exercise should be done based on five- to seven-year financial projections.
- ✓ Prior transactions in your competitive or market space can give an idea of revenue or profit multiples for valuation. However, the actual valuation and the equity given away will ultimately be a negotiation exercise.
- ✓ It's good if you can catch a wave where your venture is in a space which is the current favourite for VCs.
- ✓ Now is the best time ever to be an entrepreneur. There is more money available than fundable ideas in all the entrepreneurial hotspots of the world.
- ✓ There are strong indications that India's time has come as a favoured investment destination for VCs.
- ✓ India has government schemes available which can provide a combination of debt and equity worth exploring.
- ✓ It's generally not a good idea to take debt on to your balance sheet until you have cash flows to support the servicing of the debt.

3.

Winning with VCs

'The relationship between a start-up founder and an investor is like any marriage, blissful at its best and nightmarish when on the rocks'

—Malini Goyal, *Economic Times*

In the previous chapter, we discussed the various sources of funding, how much money should be raised and approaches for maximizing valuation at every round of funding. In this chapter, we will give you a deeper insight on a variety of issues pertaining to negotiating with VCs, which will influence the share of the wealth creation that accrues to the founders, such as the degree of control exercised by VCs and matters that can leave the founders in distress if not negotiated astutely. To keep things simple, we have used the umbrella term 'VCs', but this chapter could very well include all categories of investors, whether they are angel investors, early-stage VCs, or downstream private equity players.

When Ashok began his career in Calcutta in the field of engineering, he had to deal and negotiate with seasoned trade union leaders. Thirty years later, when he began his first dialogue with VCs, he noticed one striking similarity. The VCs, like the union leaders, had dealt with hundreds of persons like himself. The experience scale was tilted so much in the favour of the VCs or union leaders that they could have had him for lunch. Fortunately, none of them did, but he did gain know-how that can be of great value to new entrepreneurs. Ashok so far has had close dealings with five VCs and two PE players through the various rounds of funding for MindTree and Happiest Minds and also a venture he conceived two years prior to MindTree, with which he did not proceed.

If you want to get a negative view on VCs, you need not proceed further than *Tough Things First* by Ray Zinn, who bills himself as Silicon Valley's longest serving CEO. Ray sees the VCs as persons who want a return on investment (ROI) tied to an impatient time window, and when it doesn't come, are only too willing to initiate surgery to replace the heart of the company (the CEO). He also likens them to pacemakers which can quickly become defibrillators. VCs are often labelled with the unkind epithet: Vulture Capitalists. Our experience would indicate that a more appropriate epithet is 'Value Creators'. However, the 'value creation' is done in conjunction with the entrepreneur and it's important that the entrepreneur also gets his or her fair share of the value created.

Before we come to a few key pointers, Ashok would like to share the varied experiences he has had with VCs:

It was 1996, three years before I was to launch MindTree. Abhay Havaldar of Draper International sought a meeting with me. An extremely personable individual, Abhay told me about the Bill Draper Venture Fund and said that if I wanted to branch out on my own (from Wipro), they would be happy to finance me. I had an unfulfilled ambition to be an entrepreneur and in the very first meeting, I indicated that I would be interested. Things progressed with amazing swiftness. Within a couple of months, I had prepared a sketchy proposal for creating a telecom product. Abhay offered to get me a meeting with Bill. On my very next trip to the US (I used to travel about six or seven times a year), I squeezed in a meeting with Bill. We met for an hour in his elegant San Francisco office. He hardly looked at my projected numbers, but wanted to understand my commitment to entrepreneurship and motivation for making a change. He also asked me if I had any knowledge of building software products. I told him that at Wipro we had developed CyberManage, a network product, and in our computer days we had developed all our own products from the ground up, including operating systems, compilers etc. At the end of the hour, Bill told me that they would be happy to fund my venture. A week later I had a signed a term sheet for $2 million with a fifty-fifty split of equity! I readily and happily accepted it. Fortunately for me, before I could take steps to convert it into a definitive agreement, Azim Premji, my chairman, persuaded me to stay on at Wipro.

The next two years saw a lot of excitement as the dot-com boom developed. On the sidelines of NASSCOM, Som Das of Walden (an old friend from his VLSI days) arranged a breakfast meeting for me with Lip-Bu Tan, his chairman. Again, the message was the same: they would be happy to fund my venture if I chose to start on my own. A few months later, my friend, Jairaj (then industry secretary in the Karnataka government) told me he wanted me to meet someone. A lunch meeting was set-up and I knew nothing of whom I was meeting and why. It so turned out that Jairaj's aim was to be the matchmaker between V.G. Siddhartha, a VC (later to be better known as the entrepreneur behind Café Coffee Day) and myself. A few months after this meeting, I had an acceptance from Premji that we would plan for my departure from Wipro. That same evening I phoned Walden in the US and subsequently also sealed the deal with Siddhartha's firm, GTV. This time around I stated the terms and, compared to the Draper deal, was able to raise five times more while parting with about half of the equity!

Both my relationships with Walden and GTV turned out to be very, very positive. I would also say the same of the two VCs we chose at Happiest Minds, Canaan Partners and Intel. The partners all gave us a fair, maybe a generous deal (this is not to say that Draper was unfair, as I will explain later). Furthermore, they all provided value in multiple ways: they were all patient investors, struck the right balance between involvement and interference, were supportive in difficult times, came in on subsequent rounds and so on. Amongst them, for me, Lip-Bu Tan, chairman of Walden (now also chairman of Cadence), was the gold standard as a board member and for the many introductions he provided MindTree to his vast network, not limited only to his portfolio companies. In board meetings, he focused sharply on our pipeline of potential customers and always asked if there was any particular customer with whom he could provide us help. A few years after we started, Lip-Bu gifted me a copy of *Blueprint to Billion* by David Thomson and led us into the self-belief that MindTree could become a billion-dollar company.

The only negative experience (and it left me with more than a bad taste in my mouth) was when we did our second round of funding at MindTree. Towards the end of 2000, about fifteen months after we had started MindTree, we initiated a 'beauty parade' and received strong interest from every investor we had invited. One of them, the fledgling private equity arm of a giant global financial institution, made a valuation offer which was about 25 per cent higher than all the others. I had a very positive relationship with the trading arm of this institution which invested in public company shares. Quite quickly we got locked into an exclusive discussion with the company I will call VC Z. They assured us that they would move rapidly and would stipulate a very simple agreement. We then began to witness the bureaucracy of the large institution. After much delay, we received an agreement— no doubt drafted by highly paid lawyers, which I must say was the most complicated I have ever seen—providing every conceivable protection for the investor and created severe downside conditions for the founders, which never existed in our first round contracts, even when the early investors were clearly taking the bigger risk.

We spent weeks negotiating on these clauses. In the meanwhile, global recessionary storm clouds were building and the dot-com bust was manifesting. After due diligence, the investor came back with a much lower valuation and I accepted. This was not the right time for us to reopen dialogue with other investors who had shown interest. I had planned a vacation in Vienna in May 2001 with the expectation that the deal would have been long since closed. While in Vienna, I received yet another draft of the shareholders' agreement from VC Z. It still contained a clause which troubled me, but instinct told me to proceed quickly, and in consultation with Krishnakumar and Venkatraman (my CFO then and also now at Happiest Minds) I accepted it. By 4 September 2001, we had the second round money worth

$14.3 million in the bank. A week later, 9/11 occurred and the world went into a tailspin. Had we not closed the deal in early September, we may not have been able to raise a second round and MindTree could have joined the dust heap of Internet system integrators, the majority of which collapsed after the dot-com bust. The clause of which I was suspicious was later used (in my view unethically) by VC Z to wrest about 3 per cent of shareholding from MindTree, taking them from about 11 per cent to a 14 per cent holding.

Learning from Ashok's Experience

First, let us take a look at Ashok's transaction with Draper International, from which he walked away even after accepting a term sheet. This attitude was truly that of a novice at work. Ashok had no idea of what a fair valuation was for the company he wanted to create and he just accepted the first offer that came his way.

From Bill Draper's angle, the deal was quite fair and in line with his fifty-fifty philosophy articulated in his book, *The Start-up Game*: the VC puts in all the money and the founders put in 'blood, sweat and tears', and unless the amount of money is very small or very large, a fifty-fifty split is fair. Dilution for ESOPs and subsequent rounds impacts both parties equally. If Ashok had gone ahead with this deal and had to raise three to four rounds, he would have been left with a small stake and a small share of value creation, to be shared further with the other founders.

As Daniel Isenberg says in his book, *Worthless, Impossible and Stupid*, there are plenty of entrepreneurs who feel they have been short-changed or have not been able to capture an appropriate share of the value created. You don't want to be one of them.

For the first round at MindTree, though Ashok did not shop around for offers from other VCs, his co-founders had been independently searching the scene before they met him, including initiating discussions with Walden. It was evident that Walden and GTV represented the best bet and most importantly, there was a high comfort level with the managing partners—Lip-Bu Tan and Som Das of Walden and Siddhartha of GTV. Personal chemistry is very important to sustain such a relationship.

When Ashok was zeroing in on the partner for MindTree's second round, Lip-Bu did warn him that VC Z would work primarily as financial investors and that their private equity business was very small. All investors will probably claim to provide 'intelligent money'. The entrepreneur should not hesitate to demand more clarity on that—the number of introductions one can expect, forums of the VC where one can participate, and so on. In the case of VC Z, they had no leverage with their much larger parent entity, which meant no introductions to their portfolio companies, and VC Z had created no ecosystem to provide support to their investees. To make matters worse, he felt that the actions of the dealing partners were driven by their own selfish considerations (such as their bonuses) rather than what was good and fair for MindTree.

Also, Ashok had made a mistake in assuming that a great relationship with the public company equity trading arm of VC Z would translate into a successful relationship with the PE subsidiary. The trading arm was a hugely successful, experienced entity. The PE arm was new and struggling to prove itself.

As noted earlier, there is an asymmetry in the experience of VCs dealing with entrepreneurs, and vice versa. In MindTree, Ashok and the team handled the negotiations directly with no external advisory assistance. For the Happiest Minds negotiations, Ashok brought in S.R. Gopalan as an advisor to be with him while commercial agreements and valuations were discussed. Likewise, an excellent lawyer, Rajiv Khaitan, also associated with the company from an early stage so that he understood the business context well and provided advice not limited to legal agreements.

Understanding the VC's Mind

Before you approach a VC and move on to negotiations, it's important to understand the mind of the VC, the nature of their business, on what sectors they focus, etc. Publications such as *Venture Intelligence* and *VC Circle* will give you a fairly comprehensive list of investors. You should go to the particular investor's website to find out the kind of investments they have made, who are the venture partners on their board and so on.

A typical VC organization will receive thousands of deals; they will at best agree to meet a few 100 after initial scrutiny, and then go on to fund only a handful. Sudhir Sethi, managing partner of IDG India, says they received 2000-plus deals in 2015. Of these, thirty-seven were presented to the advisory team and twenty-two were approved for investment—a little over 1 per cent. The good news from these numbers is that if your proposal survives the initial screening, there is a good probability of getting funded!

Alok Mittal of Canaan feels that 95 per cent of proposals which come to VCs do not get funding. It's important for you to carefully plan so that your proposal is amongst the 1–5 per cent which succeed in getting funded.

In spite of all the filtering that VCs do, they still land upon a large number of failed projects. A large US Silicon Valley VC, which has done over 300 deals, advised us that they had lost money in one-third, had obtained a 1x to 2x return in another third, and in the balance third a small proportion at the top end had given very high returns of 10x or above. This allowed the VC to get an overall 4.5x return in the average of seven years they were vested in their ventures. Bill Draper reports that his first India fund returned 16x in six years on their limited partner money, which would make it amongst the best performing funds in India and even the world.

This backdrop will help us understand the drivers for the VCs and their thought processes. First, they are in the business of value creation and in this context, have an enormous pressure to give attractive returns to the limited partners from whom they raise funds—this has to be their prime goal. Since they are inundated with proposals, they quickly cut to the chase, so many appear impatient. However, once they choose a venture for funding, we do believe most VCs enter into these agreements with a view to building a supportive relationship. Almost every VC with whom we spoke said that the most important decision-making factors for them are the quality of the main promoters and the rest of the founding team. They know that business plans are likely to change in response to market needs and are generally sceptical of the stated numbers.

The observations above are borne out of analysing Bill Draper's approach towards Ashok. He took a positive call in just one meeting in spite of a sketchy business plan, because he assessed that Ashok had a commitment towards entrepreneurship and his track record indicated the perseverance to see through the ups and downs of an entrepreneurial venture.

Another very important consideration for VCs is to be clear about their exit from the venture, including the time frame and the modality of the same, whether it will be an IPO or a buyout or any other exit strategy. This is the mechanism through which they will do payouts to their limited partners with the money that will accrue from the venture. Keeping this in mind, in both his ventures—MindTree and Happiest Minds—Ashok committed upfront that the company would go public in a maximum of seven years from inception. This set the right expectation from the very start and there was never any pressure from the VCs to sell out the business, accelerate the IPO or seek an earlier exit.

How Much Equity Should Be Parted With?

There are two broad aspects of negotiating with VCs: what per cent of your company you're going to part with in each round, and an understanding of the clauses in often complex agreements, which can bring grief to investees in later years.

In this section, we'll focus on the commercial negotiations which will determine what per cent of the company founders will be left with by the time of the IPO or any other exit. Founders themselves should have a goal of how much of the company they want to retain at the end of the pre-IPO round. Let's illustrate this with some actual data:

Company	Promoters' Pre-IPO Holding (%)
Microsoft	77.2
Narayana Hrudayalaya	66.8
Café Coffee Day	63.3
MindTree	42.1
Apple	36.9
Google	36.1
Facebook	28.1

For all the companies in the group above, the holdings are shared between two or three persons only. The exceptions are MindTree, where there were ten co-founders, while Facebook only had a single founder. While the Facebook promoter holding is only 28.1 per cent, Mark Zuckerberg held 57.6 per cent of voting shares post the IPO, indicating his concern on retaining control. The division between the key promoter and others is also interesting. Bill Gates at 49.2 per cent was significantly ahead of Paul Allen at Microsoft. At the low end, Steve Jobs with 15 per cent was just 1 per cent ahead of Mike Markkula at Apple. While Steve Jobs was able to overtake Microsoft in creating the most valuable company in the world, he wasn't able to retain for himself a holding proportionate to his contribution. Another aspect that comes on to the table is that in the list given, the companies based in the US were able to raise large sums at IPO and yet restrict their dilution to low, single digit percentage by going public after reaching huge valuations.

To Ashok's surprise, serial entrepreneur K. Ganesh says that in his ventures, founders generally come down to a holding of 20–30 per cent pre-exit. Since all his ventures have only three founders, including his wife, as a family, this still gives them a decent share of the wealth creation.

The TV reality show *Shark Tank*, where entrepreneurs pitch their business plans before investors, gives an interesting though exaggerated dynamic on how investors often respond: They are quick to reject businesses with little differentiation. They also swiftly identify weaknesses in the entrepreneur's presentation, sometimes taking them apart in the process to make a case for a lower valuation. On the plus side, when they do see something differentiated which offers scope for ROI in a time frame of three to five years, they quickly get into the investment bidding process. In real life however, as we have seen, there is much higher emphasis on the quality of the entrepreneurial team.

Another of Ashok's experiences is that VCs like to hunt in pairs. The lead investor will typically want a 20–25 per cent holding while the second investor will expect between 10–15 per cent. With appropriate negotiation, you can restrict first round equity dilution to 25–30 per cent. You could, of course, do smaller rounds and give away less, but we feel this practice leads to too many rounds and frequent diversion of effort from growing the business to raising of money. If the founders are also planning to invest, it makes sense to put in your money in the first round because that's when the valuation is lowest and it gives you more shares to the dollar or rupee invested. VCs, with their deeper pockets, can invest through top-up funds in subsequent rounds and thereby sustain their ownership percentage if they so choose. Founders, on the other hand, will get diluted from round to round and therefore, it is important to give away as little as possible at each stage.

While time-tested negotiation processes apply here as well, Gopalan suggests the following specifically with respect to negotiating terms with VCs:

- Don't negotiate against yourself. Often the investors will ask you to revise the valuation number without giving their own number, saying that your expectation is too high. This is a technique to get you to reduce the valuation. In such cases, you should ask them to counter rather than reduce your number.
- Don't make too many points. Usually you will have two or three very strong points which you would like to project. Instead, if you try to bring in too many points, you will get attacked on your weak points and the discussions will turn against you.
- Don't take a strong position without understanding the investor's point of view.
- Don't give examples of other companies which are really not comparable.
- Be cautious of earn-out linked clauses. If there is a wide gap between the valuation offered by the VC

and the valuation expected by the entrepreneurs, the VC may offer an earn-out clause where the founders get additional shares on meeting certain performance milestones in the business. Since most business plans tend to be over-optimistic, this could be seen as a negotiating tactic from the VC which leaves you with a lower equity shareholding.

- Try to close the negotiations as fast as possible. A deal is not done till a definitive, mutually binding shareholders' agreement is signed. During the intervening period, if markets turn south, the VC is likely to suggest a downward revision of the valuation or some other clause which can reduce ownership for the founders. But if markets start booming, no one is going to offer you a higher valuation.

At Happiest Minds, Ashok personally witnessed the need to expeditiously close negotiations before any external factors can impact the same. The term sheet with Canaan had been settled and discussions were underway for the binding legal agreement. Ashok was sitting with Alok in the business centre at the Hyatt Hotel in New Delhi to progress negotiations. Suddenly news came in of the first (of many) crises in the EU. The Indian stock market dropped 500 points within the next hour or so. The mood of the discussion immediately changed. Alok (a very fair person) didn't want to change the basic terms, but he suggested that in case specified revenue milestones were not met, then Ashok would not be allowed to invest in the second tranche of the first round, which would be converted into an external investors' round, effectively reducing the percentage of Ashok's holding and increasing theirs. This situation also illustrates the asymmetric nature of a VC–entrepreneur negotiation. The VCs' vast experience with such dealings helps them to suggest esoteric clauses or bring new dimensions into the negotiation. In this case, Ashok accepted Alok's proposal, the requisite milestone was met, and an external investor only round was averted. All's well that ends well.

The Shareholders' Agreement

Coming to the specific terms of agreement, VCs often insist on certain conditions in their investment agreements which, while protecting them, can put you at a disadvantage. We will now discuss some of these.

All investment agreements by VCs will include a set of veto clauses. This means that without the approval of the investors, certain actions cannot take place. It is important to read the veto clauses carefully. Many of the clauses are reasonable: for example, preventing the company from entering into new businesses, or from availing loans beyond a certain amount, or from selling the business. These veto rights can be exercised by the investors if they don't have even a 26 per cent stake. On the other hand, certain clauses must not be accepted for inclusion. For example, if VCs want the right to appoint the CEO or terminate the CEO, this has to be a walkaway clause for the entrepreneur. You may choose to bring in a CEO if you feel you don't want to be CEO or if you want an external CEO, but that decision should be yours.

Another critical clause that VCs will insist upon is preferential liquidation rights, often together with participating rights. Liquidation preference means that in the case of an exit event, the investors get their money back first. Liquidation preference is a standard practice and not unfair because the investors are bringing in money at a much higher valuation than the ESOP/sweat equity price. However, when it comes to participation rights, it is important to understand how these work in tandem. Participation rights mean that in addition to having preferential liquidation rights for their investment in the company, the investors also get a percentage of the amount that remains in proportion to their share in the company. Effectively, they get their money back more than once, sometimes twice or even more. Since this has become a standard practice, it may be difficult for you to avoid it. However, it is essential to ask that the participation rights be restricted to the amount invested, which is otherwise called one-time participation whereby the amount that a VC can take back is restricted to twice his investment.

For example, let us take a company which receives a $1 million investment at a $5 million valuation. Technically, the VC has a 20 per cent stake. If he has unlimited participation and the company gets sold for $18 million, the investor gets the following amounts:

- His initial investment of $1 million
- 20 per cent of the $17 million that remains, or $3.4 million

So the VC gets $4.4 million from the sale proceeds which is more than the $3.6 million he should have received for his 20 per cent stake. By constraining the amount of participating rights to '1x', the amount that the VC can take away in total gets restricted to 2x their investment, should they adopt the liquidation preference route. Therefore, if the company is doing well and there is a liquidation event, the VC is incentivized to convert his preference holdings to equity, as that gives him higher returns than if the liquidation plus participation rights were enforced.

In the above example, let's evaluate the VC's returns if the participation is limited to a maximum of 1x.

Situation 1: 1x liquidation + 1x participation: the VC takes back $2 million.

Situation 2: conversion: the VC takes 20 per cent of $18 million, i.e. $3.6 million, and you get 80 per cent of the exit value which is in line with the original valuation understanding and a win-win scenario.

Another clause to be wary of is the anti-dilution clause. If such a clause is present in the investment agreement, it means that any future funding at a valuation lower than the earlier valuation would result in the earlier investors being compensated by way of additional stocks. The method of calculating such compensation can be either full ratchet or a weighted average. The weighted average method is now invariably applied in international investment agreements and is fair to both the VC and the entrepreneur. The full ratchet method is heavily weighted in favour of the VC. Accordingly, you should insist on the weighted average method.

Other clauses found in VC agreements are related to the right to exit unilaterally if over a period of time the company is not able to give the VCs a proper exit. This is effected via a clause called 'drag along', which means that after a particular period, say seven years of investment, if the VC wants to exit, he will have the right to ask the entrepreneurs also to exit along with him at the same price. This way, the new buyer gets 100 per cent control of the company. Similarly, there is a concept of 'tag along', which means that if the entrepreneur finds a buyer and wishes to sell his shares, the VC has the right to sell a proportionate amount to the buyer at the same price. (This is assuming that the VC agrees to the sale in the first place.) So, as a promoter, you cannot exit by yourself.

Typically, the entrepreneur is not allowed to sell his shares without the VC's approval. But you can negotiate for the right to sell a small percentage of your stocks without the VC's approval to meet personal needs.

We mentioned earlier about the possibility of an earn-out linked clause for additional stock to the founders. If there is such a clause, it's best to examine it from a taxation angle to ensure it doesn't create an unnecessary tax burden. One approach is that the earn-out shares can be allotted to you upfront but kept in an escrow account, with the proviso that they go into the ESOP pool if the earn-out goals are not met.

Some undefined scenarios can be used by the VC to force a revaluation. For example, at MindTree, when we negotiated an equity-linked deal (shortly after 9/11)—whereby the customer has the option to acquire a small per cent of the company upon placing orders above a minimum threshold—VC Z insisted we do a revaluation even though the structure of the equity-linked deal didn't require a fresh valuation. The shareholders' agreement was silent on this and VC Z refused consent to the equity-linked deal until a revaluation was done. What made this particularly galling and, in Ashok's view, unethical, was when we learned by accident that VC Z had informed their limited partners that a 'reset' had been implicitly agreed to by the company when there had never been any such agreement— implicit or explicit. Based on this experience, in the Happiest Minds shareholders' agreement, we included a clause that the management would not require the VC's permission for an equity-linked deal entailing up to 5 per cent of equity dilution.

Sometimes, if the VCs are not convinced about your ability to reach your goals, they may insist on milestone-based funding. This is also not a good idea but it may become unavoidable. In such a case, you must ensure that the milestones are reasonable and that you have enough money at each stage to reach the milestone. It may be worthwhile getting a commitment from the VCs on further rounds which are linked to time and not linked to milestones, where the former indicates that only if and when required, the VC will provide additional funding such that the VCs funds are not blocked and the venture does not sit on idle cash. The VCs typically keep aside a top-up provision for the next round. Accordingly, this is not a very difficult clause to be included.

Where there is more than one investor, under the same agreement the investment from all of them will come with the same conditions. Exceptions could be where one of the investors is a government fund bound by certain different rules, which is typically acceptable because the terms defined by the government are generally easier as compared to VC terms.

Disputes with VCs cannot be ruled out, so it is important to have an arbitration clause, which should be in the jurisdiction in which the company is registered. In many cases, the disputes arise because of poor performance by the company which makes the investors jittery. The investors, then, on their own may find buyers for the company. If the investor insists on fully implementing the liquidation and participation clauses, the entrepreneur may be left with nothing. Most VCs, in such situations, will give a fair share to the entrepreneur for the work done as well as the fact that he (the entrepreneur) may have to participate in the smooth handover of the company.

The Entrepreneur–VC Relationship

During the course of a venture, the entrepreneur will build many partnerships and relationships. None is as important as the relationship with the investors/VCs.

There are multiple cases where relationships turn sour and in such cases, more often than not, it is the entrepreneur who loses out. Across the world, there are deals worth hundreds of millions of dollars mired in litigation.

In an article titled 'Start-ups Sold, with the Founders Left Out' by Stephen M. Davidoff (*International Herald Tribune*, 2 May 2013), Davidoff writes that many entrepreneurs are cut a bad deal, particularly when a company is sold. They illustrated this argument through the case of Bloodhound Technologies, a company which developed fraud monitoring software. The company raised $5 million in two rounds of funding in 1999 and 2000. When the dot-com bubble burst, the company ran into turbulence. The investors fired the founders and rebuilt the company with a management team of their choice. A few years later, the investors were able to sell the company for $82.5 million, the new management team was paid a bonus of $15 million, and the original investors received $36,000 collectively amongst them!

Even sadder is the story of Sandy Lerner and Leonard Bosack who co-founded Cisco in 1984 and raised $2.6 million while parting with 30 per cent of the company. They agreed to a four-year vesting period at the end of which they would have 90 per cent of the founder's stock. But before the stock could vest, Lerner was fired and Bosack resigned soon after, leaving them no share of the billions which were to be made later.

It is precisely to avoid situations of this sort happening to you that we have advised close attention to the boundary conditions of clauses protecting investor interests. Founders may also want to insist on some clauses which will define their rights.

Notwithstanding the above cases of strife between entrepreneurs and VCs, it is our belief that an overwhelming majority of such relationships turn out to be win-win partnerships. Having taken reasonable precautions such as reference checks (with other entrepreneurs) on the VCs you want to go with and also careful scrutiny of the shareholders' agreement, it's best to enter into the relationship with a spirit of trust and confidence.

Another aspect of the relationship is the degree of involvement of the VC. There is a fine line between involvement and interference. Also, what is acceptable to one entrepreneur may not be okay for another. For example, at Happiest Minds, one of our VCs suggested a monthly update via teleconference. Ashok politely said that such a call could transpire between him and our CEO, while Ashok would engage with the investors through a detailed quarterly board meeting. On the other hand, some entrepreneurs are happy with such an arrangement and welcome even a weekly interaction with the VC.

All of the six VC relationships that Ashok has had have been very positive. Even in the case of VC Z mentioned earlier, Ashok felt MindTree made the wrong choice, and in spite of the one major incident, the relationship itself was very cordial. Ashok's view is that the trigger for discord is when the VC's investments go underwater; the best way to ensure a happy relationship is to deliver broadly on your commitments, acknowledging that some slips will occur during the journey.

K. Ganesh has had fifteen VC relationships and all of them have been very positive. He believes the secret lies in honesty, transparency and constant communication.

One last word of advice on this matter. Don't hold back or suppress bad news. Let it surface quickly and make the VC your partner in trying to find a solution.

KEY TAKEAWAYS

✓ A very small percentage (1–5 per cent) of proposals which reach VCs get funded. You have to do your homework well to ensure that your project is one of those selected for funding.

✓ The first step is to understand the mind, motivation and drivers for the VC. In spite of the huge filtering process, VCs still find one-third of projects they've invested in failing and another third giving only marginal returns. The VC's three main criteria for selection are the idea, the market and the team. Above all else, VCs take a bet on people and it's the team which counts. VCs also need to have an upfront understanding of how and when they will get their exit.

✓ You should also research the VCs you are approaching. Meet other portfolio companies to assess how much support they provide and their behaviour in difficult times. Is their money truly 'intelligent' money? Don't just accept the first offer you receive for funding.

✓ Entrepreneurship is all about value creation through a partnership between the investor and the entrepreneur. It is important that you get your appropriate share of the rewards. Too many entrepreneurs find they have short-changed themselves by giving away too much equity. Founders should have a goal of retaining at least 40 per cent of the equity at the pre-IPO stage. A key contributor to going above 40 per cent is if the founders also put in their money—in effect, become their own VC.

✓ The process of bringing in an external investor is not only one of parting with some ownership, but also one of ceding control. Shareholders' agreements are complex documents designed primarily to protect the interests of investors, including defining areas where they have veto rights. The VC–entrepreneur relationship is asymmetric because VCs have experience of negotiating and dealing with hundreds of entrepreneurs, while you will have at best a few such experiences in your lifetime.

Accordingly, it's best to retain an advisor to help you through these negotiations.

✓ It is inevitable that the shareholders' agreement will have clauses like 'tag along' rights and preferential liquidation rights. While this is seemingly okay, the devil lies in the details and it is the boundary conditions of these clauses which are important to protect the entrepreneur's interests.

✓ You, the entrepreneur, should also be clear upfront about what clauses are not acceptable to you. For example, the right to appoint or terminate the CEO should never be with the VCs. Also, VCs should not have the right to force a sale of the company unless the entrepreneurs have been unable to provide an exit in a promised period and an IPO doesn't look feasible.

✓ Sometimes VCs may suggest 'exotic' or unusual clauses like earn-outs or an investor-only round if conditions are not met. Look out for unintended consequences of such clauses, including tax implications and also the impact of these on ownership.

✓ Entrepreneurs seldom ask for special clauses which remove ambiguities regarding their freedom to make choices. Such clauses could include the right to enter into an equity-linked deal entailing up to, say, 5 per cent of equity dilution. While acquisitions are typically an area where VCs have veto rights, the CEO can request for allowing freedom to decide on small, strategic acquisitions.

✓ The VC relationship is the most important one you will make in your entrepreneurial journey. While safeguarding your own interest, enter into it with a positive approach and invest in making the relationship successful.

4.

Mission, Vision, Values and Culture

'Culture eats strategy for breakfast'

—Peter Drucker

We agree with Peter Drucker on the importance of culture. A shared vision helps align actions within a company. All business strategy differentiators have a shelf life and your company's culture can be your most important and long-lasting differentiator. We also believe that strongly internalized mission, vision and values (MVV) are the most important prerequisites for the development of a vibrant, positive and supportive culture.

Articulating a set of MVV statements is not likely to be a top priority for a start-up CEO as the team is under 24x7 pressure to define and develop the products and services they need to take to market and win over customers—i.e. establishing the business's lifeline. However, the mission, vision and values are foundational musts which define collectively the reason for a company's existence and the characteristics of the company you are seeking to create. The mission and values should be able to last the lifetime of the company, though the mission statement may need to be changed if the business model has to be radically transformed in response to strategic considerations. We emphasize the importance of the MVV being internalized and senior leaders walking the talk on them, otherwise these undertakings become meaningless. Unfortunately, many leaders that do define the mission, vision and values for their companies don't take any steps for internalizing these, with the result that these remain only on paper.

Ashok recollects addressing the annual function of the India development centre of a large MNC. The theme was 'becoming the best offshore development centre'. Before imparting his 'advice', Ashok, as is his wont, began with a few questions to the audience. The first question he asked was, 'How many of you recollect your company's mission statement?' The next was, 'Do you remember your company's values?' Not a single hand went up. Ashok was not surprised. He had read the MVV prior to the talk. It comprised long sentences and it was evident that they were articulated in a remote land and not addressed to the audience he was addressing. Also, there appeared to be no programme to turn these statements into living, energizing, aspirational and inspirational statements indicating the type of culture the company wanted to build. Instead, it seemed that someone in corporate communications had done a wordsmithing exercise.

This case took Ashok back to his experience with how the MVV had evolved in MindTree and how Ashok had used that learning to get it right the first time round in Happiest Minds. In his own words:

My co-founders at MindTree included, thanks to Subroto Bagchi, three founders from Cambridge Technology

Partners (CTP) in the US. They in turn attracted some of their colleagues from CTP and the key members of the US office were all ex-CTP. This team brought in significant consulting capabilities which enabled MindTree to compete against Scient, Viant, CTP and many other US e-system integrators rather than the larger Indian IT companies (at least for the duration that the dot-com boom lasted). However, the US team in unison would reject almost everyone we sent from India with the angry reaction of: 'Why the hell have you sent XYZ to the US?' These were competent persons and though they lacked consulting skills, they did bring in other capabilities which the Cambridge crowd didn't recognize. The situation got really alarming when they unanimously rejected a co-founder who headed one of our business units—the person we had decided would be our senior person based in the US. It was true that this particular leader didn't have the suavity, polish and smooth articulation of the CTP team. What they didn't appreciate were the many other strengths this leader possessed. Ultimately, I was able to get this leader accepted. The stratagem and approach I took for this is another story. The point here is that cultural differences were leading to a lot of friction and instead of one consolidated team, we had a US team and an India team. Furthermore, we found a lot of difference in the expectations on empowerment, authority and delegation from the US team's side, while I felt that many proposals for investment came without adequate depth and homework.

To make matters worse, the dot-com market was slowing down and some finger-pointing had already begun. In the midst of all this, we invited Jukka Laitamaki, professor of marketing at Fordham College, New York, to

India for a training programme. During one of the sessions, I asked Jukka how he managed cultural differences which seem to pull the organization apart in so many different directions. Jukka's response was an eye-opener for me. First, he said, 'Never think of culture as something to be managed, but to be evolved. Also, don't think of cultural differences as a problem, but something to be celebrated as a source of new ideas and different ways of doing things. What is important is for people to be aligned behind the same values to move the organization ahead in unison.' His next question was, 'What are the values of MindTree?' We were a young company at the time and the entire senior and middle management of the company were in the room. I asked who would like to volunteer a response to Jukka's question. Not a single hand went up. Ultimately, Subroto, the author of the original values, went up to the board and wrote them out.

It was evident that if no one had a clue what the values were, we couldn't even begin the journey of internalizing them. Within a few days, we began a participatory process involving all 500 MindTree minds to redefine our values. We had small group discussions across the world and, through my personal communication newsletter called 'Snapshots', I invited all to contribute towards what they felt MindTree stood for and what they wanted it to stand for. As the responses poured in, our main values, which were to be later called our CLASS values (Caring, Learning, Achieving, Sharing and Social Responsibility) just jumped out at us. For internalization, I personally addressed all new entrants within ninety days of their joining on the CLASS values in a very interactive session. This was supplemented by an excellent booklet on integrity failures created by Subroto. There was so much pride in the CLASS values that I was surprised when MindTree modified them after I left—perhaps the values were associated excessively with me? Hopefully, the new values are serving them well.

The Happiest Minds MVV

At Happiest Minds, the mission, vision and values, together with the name of the company, all come together holistically around a central theme of happiness:

Mission: Happiest People. Happiest Customers

Values: Sharing, Mindful, Integrity, Learning, Excellence, Social Responsibility
(The values lend themselves to an appropriate acronym: SMILES.)

Five-year Vision:

- Be the Happiness Evangelists for each other, our customers and society.
- Achieve a very successful IPO in FY 2020.
- Be known as the company with the highest standards of corporate governance.
- Be recognized for thought leadership in our focused areas of technology and solutions.
- Be a leader in social responsibility initiatives.

Each vision component is supported by measurement criteria.

There is a lot of focus on social responsibility as research shows that happiness is highest in moments of giving. We call our landmarks, such as a first profitable quarter or achieving $50 million of revenue, 'smilestones'. We commemorate every smilestone by gifting meals in the name of our team members and customers to the Mid Day Meal Programme for poor schoolchildren. We have set a goal of contributing 1 million meals by the time of the IPO and, at the time of writing this book, have already crossed 690,000 meals. Even the logo of Happiest Minds is a symbol of the being, belonging and becoming of a Happiest Person.

The values contain one word, 'mindful', which you are unlikely to find in the value statement of other companies. We believe so much in being mindful that we have added a tagline to our logo identifying us as the mindful IT company, which is a logical extension of our brand positioning of happiness.

All of the above-mentioned values are backed by many communication platforms where the values are visited often by the chief people officer, Raja Shanmugam, the CEO & MD, Sashi Kumar, and Ashok. We have developed multiple practices and rituals to reinforce the happiness theme, including a 360° feedback for all, including myself, on whether we live by the values.

We believe that our MVV has created enormous pride in our teams and contributed hugely to the Happiest Minds culture. Visiting delegations and customers show considerable interest in what they see as a refreshingly different approach. In fact, the idea of describing ourselves as the 'Mindful IT Company' came through Lynda Leonard of the Information Technology Association of Canada. At an IT industry conference in

Toronto, which Ashok was addressing, she introduced him as the chairman of 'the mindful IT company'.

Creating a Great Place to Work

An important contributor to creating a great company culture is consciously trying to create a great place to work. For Ashok, the best framework to follow is the one developed by the Great Places to Work (GPTW) Institute, a global organization which operates in fifty countries and surveys 7000 companies and 2 million team members of these companies every year. Prasenjit Bhattacharya, the India head of the GPTW, has a passion for enabling the creation of great places to work, and lives, breathes and dreams the subject almost like entrepreneurs do.

There are two major components to the survey: The trust index©, which ascertains 'what employees experience and say' and a culture audit, which assesses 'what managers say and do'.

The trust index© classifies responses into five major areas:

- Credibility
- Respect
- Fairness
- Pride
- Camaraderie

There is also a capstone question which asks team members selected at random whether they consider their company a 'great place to work'.

The culture audit assesses nine areas of people practice:

- Hiring and welcoming
- Inspiring
- Speaking

- Listening, collaborating and grievance redressal
- Thanking
- Developing
- Caring (balancing, supporting, including)
- Celebrating
- Sharing (rewarding and contributing)

When we started Happiest Minds, Prasenjit told Ashok that we had created a big challenge for ourselves by selecting the name. He said it would raise very high expectations and raise the bar for us in terms of being seen as a 'great place to work' since responses, though measured in absolute numbers, are driven by expectations. He was correct. In the early days, if any announcement didn't delight the team, we would get a chorus of 'this doesn't make me happy'. We reset the expectations by communicating that the name of our company and the first part of our mission statement, 'Happiest People', didn't mean that it was our job to make every employee happy all the time. Happiness is an individual choice and we were meant to play a catalysing role to enable the team's happiness. On the other hand, the second part of the mission statement, 'Happiest Customers', was a collective promise from all of us.

Once the above message got through, we found both our GPTW ratings and also Glassdoor ratings showed a healthy rise. For Glassdoor in particular, we found our ratings went above our comparison group, which included the largest IT services companies. In our third year, we made it to the top five emerging companies in the GPTW list, and the following year we were able to register a further 6 per cent point increase in our rating as a 'great place to work'—a mountain of a jump in one year, according to Prasenjit.

Even if you don't find yourself as a ranked company in the GPTW list, there is great value in participating in the GPTW assessment to learn from the feedback, and also to assess your own culture as you prepare the culture audit document.

The Challenges of Creating a Great Company Culture

A great culture is not a mechanical output you can expect from a box into which you feed the right inputs and install the right processes. There is every likelihood that the culture which evolves in your company is quite different from the culture you intended to create. Firstly, people come into the company from a variety of backgrounds with their own set of experiences and leadership styles. It's not unlikely that subcultures will develop within different business units. This itself is fine as long as these subcultures are all in consonance with what we would call the 'mother' culture—that of the company as a whole. Cultures will also change from time to time based on external challenges. A sudden dip in the fortunes of the company is like a stress test for the company culture—some will demonstrate resilience, while others will become dysfunctional and disintegrate. All cultures will exhibit elements of toxicity at some time or in pockets. It is our experience that the best way to address such situations is to acknowledge the problem and tackle it head-on. The problem will not disappear if you are in denial or allow it to simmer or look the other way.

Though it is a cliché, senior leadership must 'walk the talk' and be role models for the values and type of culture the company wants to evolve. For example, let us assume you want to develop a culture which is collaborative with a high degree of commitment and accountability. When you bring in a group of highly competitive and ambitious leaders, their natural tendency is to grow their own empires or protect their own turf. Collaboration is unlikely to be a personal priority.

The company then has to set up mechanisms and programmes to facilitate collaboration. The company's rewards and recognitions programme must be tuned towards celebrating behaviour which indicates a strong adherence to your company values. In terms of goals, our approach is to define company level objectives and cascade downwards with individual goals for each person.

Raja Shanmugam, who supported by Happiness Evangelist Sharon Andrew, has contributed enormously to the Happiest Minds' culture, recommends the following for developing a positive culture:

- Define mission, vision and values early. Build a community of shared vision—people may have different personalities and even different personal agendas, but as long as they align with the organization vision you can build synergy.
- Create an expectation early of what kind of culture you would like for to thrive—organizations are about people.
- Enforce company values through role modelling by leadership.
- Articulate 'what is encouraged' and 'what will not be tolerated' and act on these policies stringently.
- Get basics in place early. Policies, evaluation systems, rewards and recognitions, compensation and benefits, knowledge management, leadership and development, information systems—these are critical to put in place and run smoothly as early as possible, so the organization can take them as a given and focus on the larger external differentiators. The absence of these will be hugely disorienting.
- Build emotional infrastructure—this is extremely helpful in building trust and interpersonal connects at

the leadership level and ensuring commitment of the
employees at an operational level.

- Build a social connect in the organizational goals—
being engaged in a higher purpose is a great motivator
and a wonderful alignment tool.
- Set challenging goals—high-performing individuals
need to be satisfied that the mountain is worth climbing
before embarking on the climb.

Approaches as laid out by Raja Shanmugam above have led
to Happiest Minds being in the top quadrant of the GPTW's
2016 culture audit, with seven of our practices classified as 'Best
Culture'.

We would also recommend that it's important to let your
culture grow and develop its own characteristics before you
think of grafting other cultures on to it. To facilitate this, we
would not recommend acquisitions in the first three or four
years of a company's life. We are surprised at the number of
companies which get into M & A mode very early in their
existence, only to end up with a strong culture mismatch.

We all like to call our companies and teams 'families'—this
includes companies that, at the drop of a hat, lay off or terminate
a significant number of their organization. Ashok admits that
he himself continuously emphasizes the 'family'—be it the
MindTree family or the Happiest Minds family or the Dawn
Consulting family. In order to retain credibility, the behaviour
of those who call their companies 'family' must also be like that
of a family member. It should be a declared policy that lay-
offs will be a last resort and preferably never done. That said,
we must also see the inevitable difference between the way we
would treat an unsuccessful family member as compared to a
non-performing colleague in our pseudo-families. You would
not expel or disown an unsuccessful family member. But in the

case of a non-performing manager, it would be unfair to the organization and your colleagues if a separation is not enacted after all attempts to help the team member have failed. In fact, lack of action would also be unfair to the concerned team member who could go elsewhere and perform better in another setting. Acknowledging such differences between a real family and your company as a family is also necessary to retain credibility.

Even in such situations, in a family scenario where the company is under stress because someone has been asked to leave, Ashok has taken the approach of giving managers and leaders (particularly senior or older ones) extra notice, double or even more than the required notice in the appointment letter, so that they can get a new job even while they are in their current employment. Extended notice has been given even for younger or junior team members, though this is mostly not needed as they are able to get jobs quite quickly in an industry which has high growth and high attrition levels.

KEY TAKEAWAYS

✓ Culture can be your most unique and enduring differentiator which other companies can't replicate as easily.

✓ Mission, vision and values (MVV) play an important role in defining the type of culture you want to create. The MVV statements must be consistent with each other and should be simple, inspirational and aspirational. To translate these statements into reality, the MVV must be internalized and senior leaders must be role models.

✓ Cultural differences in different parts of the organization should not be seen as a problem but as a source of new ideas and a different way of doing things. The organization is to be aligned through shared values and constructed as moving in the same direction through a shared vision.

✓ Another contributor to creating a great organizational culture is consciously trying to create a 'great place to work'.

✓ Subcultures are likely to evolve within your organization, which is fine, as long as they are in consonance with and do not subvert the 'mother culture'.

✓ Cultures have a way of evolving in a manner which can surprise you, even if you have fed in the appropriate inputs.

✓ Cultures can turn toxic from time to time and some pockets of toxicity will emerge occasionally. Denial or looking the other way will not help. It's best to quickly recognize the problem and identify root causes. Sometimes the problem is one of perception, in which case the solution is as simple as oft-repeated communication to change the perception. In many other cases, even external help may be required to address the issue.

✓ High-achievement-oriented leaders see themselves in competition with other such leaders and it is not in their natural wavelength to collaborate. Mechanisms are needed to increase organizational collaboration.

✓ The company's reward and recognition scheme also signals what the leadership considers important and thereby influences culture. It is not enough to recognize only high performance. There can be awards for collaboration, innovation, empathy or social responsibility.

✓ It is best to avoid M & A activity for the first three to four years of a company's life. Different companies have different cultures, even though some may appear similar. A 'too early' M & A is like grafting another culture on to your own even before it has taken firm root.

✓ Don't just call your company and team a family without being able to demonstrate this through the way you behave, particularly in difficult times. Lay-offs should definitely be seen as a last resort. If a 'family' member has to be let go for non-performance, it should be handled with empathy so the person makes a soft landing.

5.

Building Your Organization

'An organization, no matter how well designed, is only as good as the people who live and work in it'

—Dee Hock

'Good corporate governance is about "intellectual honesty" and not just sticking to rules and regulations; capital flows towards companies that practice this type of good governance'

—Mervyn King

Everything You Need to Know about Setting up a Founding Team

In this chapter, we will address the many questions about the basic structural set-up that we hear from young or potential entrepreneurs: How many founders should we have? Should the founders know each other from before? Should they have similar or diverse backgrounds? How do you fix founders' compensation? How do you divide equity between founders?

What happens when a founder doesn't measure up? What leads to conflict between founders?

One response we often give upfront is that for many of the questions there is no one right or wrong answer. The best approach must take into consideration the players involved and be fine-tuned according to the situation.

Our experience with most entrepreneurial teams we have encountered is that two or more people who have studied together or worked together previously usually decide to embark on a start-up together. Single-founder set-ups are infrequent. In principle there is nothing against having a solitary founder, but investors do like to bet on teams and reduce overdependence on one individual. Also, we believe it helps to dream a dream together which requires two or more people in the founding team. There are amazing success stories of duos who have founded entities together: Larry Page/Sergey Brin at Google and Bill Gates/Paul Allen at Microsoft globally and in our own backyard, we had the Bansal duo at Flipkart and the Bahl–Bansal duo at Snapdeal. We feel somewhat larger founding teams help in being supportive of each other when things are not going well or when someone on the team is experiencing doubts. Naveen Tewari of InMobi expresses a similar sentiment. The founding team there comprised four friends who had studied together, and Naveen says that the power of four kept them going. Narayana Murthy felt he needed seven founders for Infosys, MindTree had ten, and Happiest Minds a full cricket team of eleven.

Narayana Murthy consciously chose persons who had worked with him and also persons with complementary capabilities. However, in many cases, founders who have been friends in school or have worked together tend to have similar skills and there is confusion on what roles each will play.

Ashok describes how the founding teams at MindTree and Happiest Minds were selected:

When my co-founders at MindTree approached me through Walden, Subroto had already lined up eight founders. Later I was to bring in the tenth founder, Janakiraman [Jani], to head the engineering business—but he could also have been Subroto's choice, except that at the time, the team had only been looking at Internet solutions. Subroto had done an excellent job of lining up the team. He first spoke to Krishnakumar, then CEO of Wipro's e-commerce division, and reporting to me. He then approached several persons who had worked with him in the engineering division at Wipro and one other person who was part of his current team in Lucent. Since Subroto approached those whom he considered the best among those he had worked with, we did end up with an A-team. The masterstroke was to add three founders from Cambridge Technology Partners in New Jersey. Anjan Lahiri, earlier in Wipro, moved to the US and Subroto had remained in touch with him. Anjan was able to bring on board with him two of his colleagues—Scott Staples and Kamran Ozair.

While this was a top-notch set of individuals with unique skills, the roles for all were not apparent and we had to do some 'force-fitting' in line with the organization's needs. We also had to go out and hire heads for finance and people practices, who had not come in as co-founders. Looking back, I think that was inequitable as these are two key roles which I feel should be headed by founders, unless you have just two or three founders.

When we started Happiest Minds, I decided the senior-most positions must be filled by founders. This included the CEO & MD, business unit CEOs, COOs and three of the most important corporate functions: people, finance and quality. I put together a mix of persons who had worked with me at MindTree, some of whom I approached and others who approached me to join the new venture. What was gratifying was that I got two co-founders from Wipro who reached out to me after my announcement of the launch. For the quality function, I was keen on getting a person from Infosys to inculcate their best practices. Through a contact, I was able to get in touch with Raja Sekher who I had never personally known or worked with. Through the above process we managed to get a fairly diverse team.

At both MindTree and Happiest Minds, I saw the value of a large founding team due to the additional passion and commitment that comes from being a founder. I also developed a philosophy that the senior-most persons who have the most crucial roles and will also contribute the most to wealth creation must come in as founders with higher stock than other department heads. Accordingly, I am not in favour of a model when a bunch of techies come together as founders and divide the founders' sweat equity amongst themselves, while persons who occupy more crucial roles come in later without founder status.

Let's come now to the question of how founders should be compensated and how equity should be divided amongst them. A small minority of founders do opt for equal or somewhat egalitarian sharing. Two examples of equal sharing, which have worked out well in two-founder scenarios, come to mind. The first is Google, which has equal sharing between Larry Page and Sergey Brin. The second is OSSCube, an open systems focused IT services company. The two founders of OSSCube,

Lavanya Rastogi and Vineet Agarwal, have done two ventures together and in both cases decided to split equity fifty-fifty, with the philosophy that they would not measure what each was contributing. However, these are exceptional cases; it is the view of most VCs and as well as ours that different founders create differing value for the company and equity should be shared in the broad proportion of expected value addition, with the CEO getting double of the CXO level. At MindTree, Ashok did opt for an egalitarian approach as he had a pre-selected team while he decided on a model of wider disparity at Happiest Minds. A start-up cannot afford the salary that founders were earning at their most recent jobs. Inevitably, founders have to take salary cuts and those with the highest stock should take the highest percentage of salary cuts. At both MindTree and Happiest Minds, Ashok would have taken a salary cut of above 50 per cent while the other three internal board members at MindTree would have taken 20–30 per cent smaller cuts. The most amazing instance of adopting low founder salaries is Infosys, with Narayana Murthy setting the example by keeping his own salary very low. This continued even when Infosys had become a highly profitable, multibillion-dollar entity. Narayana Murthy's reasoning was that the founders would be rewarded on performance through dividends on stock. At MindTree, the founders' salary was kept much lower than market rates till the IPO. After that, there was internal pressure to remove this gap in the pay scale, profit commission and perquisites. At Happiest Minds, the gap between founder salaries and the market is smaller (partly because living costs have gone up so much), but Ashok visualizes that this gap will be bridged once the company reaches around $200 million. The bottom line, though, is that founders do need to make a sacrifice on compensation for several years. High founder salaries are also a red flag for VCs.

Some wonder whether founders merit a special role or status because they are the founders of the company. Ashok maintains the firm view that being a founder is not a role and neither does it entitle you to being favoured for any role in preference to a better qualified claimant within the company. He sees the founders as a team that has come together to take the entrepreneurial risk of creating a successful venture for which they are also prepared to make sacrifices. For this, they must get a generous share of rewards when the venture succeeds. However, being a founder does not give any person any other entitlement in operational matters. For example, at MindTree there was one founder who was not at a CXO level. He was capable, dedicated and passionate. Ashok did not include him in the executive council (EC) and some of the other founders felt Ashok was being unfair on him. But to Ashok's mind the issue was very black and white. Would the founder's role at MindTree have merited his being on the EC and would his inclusion have been suggested even if he had not been a founder? All founder-related decisions must be purely merit-based. If not, there is a big danger of the team harbouring resentment against the founders that there is favouritism and that the only people who matter in the company are the founders. Notwithstanding the above, being a founder is a matter of legitimate pride for a person. It is perfectly fair if, in addition to their designations, founders also add 'co-founder' to their titles, as this is a fact of the company's history.

Ashok recalls that shortly after he started MindTree, Sanjiv Aggarwal (now a VC at Helion) dropped by to meet him. At that time Sanjiv was the founding CEO of Daksh and wanted to bounce off a few thoughts. One of his questions was: how would you handle the case of a founder who is not growing commensurate to the demands of the role? A few years later, the COO of one of India's leading travel portals asked Ashok: what would you do about a founder who is excellent in his work, but whose behaviour is dysfunctional in terms of the way he deals with his team? Ashok's response in the case of non-performance was that there should be no concessions or considerations for a person on account of his or her being a founder. If all help has been provided to the individual and non-performance continues, there is no option except to ask the founder to step down. Regarding the excellent performer with dysfunctional behaviour, Ashok suggested the set-up of a counselling programme to help the individual to change, not because he or she was a founder but because this approach should be taken for any similar situation in the company. One word of caution: it is extremely difficult to change human behaviour; the first step is for the concerned person to accept the need for change and agree to making the 'change management' programme open and visible to his team.

Another common question we get is: how to prevent founder conflict and how to prevent damage to the organization in case it does occur? While there may often be very strong differences of opinion between founders, the good news is that organization-threatening founder conflict is an infrequent occurrence. The relatively few cases which occur hit the headlines. Sometimes parting between one or more founders may occur for very sensible reasons. The departing founder may have decided that he or she is not cut out for the demands of entrepreneurship. Another may realize that his or her goals in life are not aligned with the venture. In such cases, it is best to work out an amicable parting and let the departing persons get on with their life. If there is a big disagreement on strategy, the CEO's decision must be accepted. Even if a founder disagrees strongly, once the decision is taken, it must be given complete support. If a founder cannot reconcile to the decision, it is best to move on rather than foster an environment where the organization will amplify any negative signals and say that the founders don't get along or don't see eye to eye. This leads to an unhealthy grapevine and toxic culture. Some of the VCs we have worked with say that splits in the founding team are mostly linked to individual ambitions of aspiring to be CEO or some other role which is not available. Fortunately, by the time this happens, the organization may have grown enough so that one or two senior departures won't matter.

We have devoted a lot of space to this section on founders because the foundation of the company depends on them, and it is their duty and responsibility to create the right base for the company's future success.

Governance and the Statutory Board

It is important for all start-ups to follow the highest standard of corporate governance and establish this as a way of life for the entire entrepreneurial journey. We regard the statutory board of directors as the main guardians of governance, which goes well beyond compliance checklists and includes ethics in business, integrity of data, policies on discrimination, sexual harassment, whistle-blowers, etc. *Fortune India* runs an entrepreneurial recognition platform called '40 under 40' and its former head of desk and editor in charge of the '40 under 40' programme, Tanmoy Goswami, is passionate about entrepreneurship. Yet, he is appalled by the poor governance he sees in companies they evaluate. According to him, exaggerated numbers in financial performance with a view to generating hype, getting favourable media coverage and higher valuations is commonplace across sectors. Other aspects of poor governance include negative selling, disparaging comments on competition, and not making a clear distinction between company assets and personal expenditure.

Gopalan, who has served on many start-up boards, feels the ideal size of a start-up statutory board is from three to five members. If there are two VCs, each will want a seat on the board, so the committee can be supplemented with two directors from the company. An independent director, preferably with a finance background and appointed by mutual consent, is a good idea. At Happiest Minds, this was the approach decided towards corporate governance where Gopalan came on as the independent director.

Ashok's view is that investors make excellent directors. VCs have their skin in the game and an understanding of the challenges of start-ups. The main difference between his approach and that of the VCs is that they are quick on the trigger to suggest the firing of a person when results fall short of plan. In MindTree, one of the business units (BUs) faced considerable competitive headwinds. In three or probably four of the seven years prior to the IPO, it was well behind the plan. The VCs demanded the head of the particular business unit CEO more than once. Ashok's view was that the team was taking on aggressive targets and penal action of this sort would lead to people scaling down targets. Also, in two years there were external extenuating circumstances. Furthermore, it was unlikely MindTree would get a replacement who could match the incumbent's commitment, passion and flair for teamwork. Fortunately, the board deferred to Ashok's judgement and the BU performance improved over the next few years. The danger in such situations is that a CEO may hesitate to take a strong enough stand out of fear that his or her own position may be threatened. Ashok has always had the view that the companies he leads even in start-up mode should be run with governance structures comparable to public limited companies. This includes instituting board committees such as an internal audit committee, compensation committee and grievance committee. Only the Big Four (earlier Big Five) were chosen as statutory auditors. He also appointed reputed internal auditors from inception, though this is not required for a private limited company till it reaches a revenue of Rs 200 crore. We believe appointing internal auditors is essential for your own protection. Things can easily spin out of control if someone is not regularly examining your key processes and systems to see if adequate controls, checks and balances exist.

Finally, we believe that succession planning for the CEO is very much a part of a start-up board's governance responsibility. Succession planning at a very early stage may sound strange to some. However, it is often in the early stages of a company that excessive dependence exists on one key individual, usually the CEO, and it is imperative to have an agreed succession plan in the event of any emergency or unanticipated situation that leads to the CEO's departure.

When MindTree began, Ashok felt that no one in the team was ready to succeed him as chairman and CEO. In concurrence with his internal board members, Ashok named three potential successors and presented the panel to the board. He then personally contacted the preferred choice, explained the company background and ascertained whether the person would be willing to take on the mantle if approached by the board in the event of a contingency. About five years later, Ashok approached the board again to say that the external succession plan was no longer required. The board then agreed on an internal succession plan which was implemented later. Alternatively at Happiest Minds, a consensus exists with the board on an external chairman of the board (not executive chairman) to succeed Ashok in an exigency. The preferred person has conveyed his acceptance even while expressing his hopes that such a fallback plan will not be needed.

Choosing the CEO

The most important role in a company is that of the CEO. We firmly believe that one of the founders should be the company CEO, unless the founders individually and collectively feel no one amongst them is ready to be CEO and choose to look outside for one. Some of the most successful companies in the world were founder–CEO-led for many years, including Microsoft, Facebook and Infosys. When several founders come together, there has to be absolute clarity on who the 'boss' is, and that person becomes the CEO. In an interview conducted by Indulekha Aravind (*Economic Times*, 4 October 2015), while recounting his experience of bringing together seven founders, Narayana Murthy said that there has to be one undisputed boss. At Infosys, it was clear, he said, that whenever there was a difference of opinion, it was him, Narayana Murthy, who would decide.

Having become CEO at the age of thirty-four, Ashok has been a CEO for more than half his life. These are his thoughts on the role:

The word 'boss' carries a lot of negative connotations, but I agree completely with Narayana Murthy on the need for an undisputed leader. However, I hated it when most of the India-based co-founders at MindTree, while referring to me in the third person, would use the word 'boss'. For Krishnakumar (K.K.), this continued even after he became CEO and I became executive chairman! I also agree with Narayana Murthy that the CEO, as the boss, is the one who takes the major decisions, presumably after hearing out all stakeholders and opinions. Accordingly, it is the CEO who is totally accountable for results. Though it is a cliché, it is right to say that the buck stops with the CEO.

But this position can get muddied up when an executive chairman is cast as a separate role from the CEO. At Happiest Minds, I began as executive chairman. It was settled with the board that the CEO would have complete responsibility and accountability for achieving annual results. For this, he would need to be given the freedom, support and wherewithal to lead the business which, hopefully, we have done. As executive chairman, I have the responsibility of guiding Happiest Minds towards its five-year vision.

There is a lot to be said about what makes for a good CEO. It could be the subject of a full book, which I may attempt at some stage. At this time, I would simply like to say that the most important role for a CEO is to plan for his or her succession. Let me drive this point home with the story of how I became chairman and CEO of MindTree and what I did about my succession planning. As noted earlier, my co-founders chanced on me through Walden with whom they were in discussion and who had already committed funding to me. At that time, Subroto and K.K. were in dialogue for several months and had not been able to decide who would be the CEO. When I agreed that we could merge our separately planned ventures into one, there was never any doubt that I would be chairman and CEO. Subroto confided in me that MindTree would have been stillborn as K.K. and he were unable to decide on who would be CEO. Years later, when I had to implement my succession plan, I chose K.K. as CEO while nominating Subroto as vice chairman, thus paving the way for his becoming chairman. The CEO succession took place during my tenure, while the chairman succession happened after I decided to leave MindTree. K.K. went on to become a good CEO and Subroto, likewise, was the better choice for the chairman role. All in all, you could call this a 'horses for courses' solution.

Parties Who Can Help with Foundation Building

Apart from internal auditors, other entities/persons who can help you in building your organization are the advisory board, consultants and mentors.

Again, Ashok describes in his own words his experience with external expertise at Happiest Minds:

I didn't turn to the expertise of external consultants in my MindTree start-up days. At Happiest Minds, I was entirely on my own when I announced the creation of the company a few days after I had stepped down from MindTree. Accordingly, I felt the need for consultants in multiple areas, including the preparation of financial and marketing plans for the VCs, negotiation with the VCs and the formulation of all the legal details in starting a company, including complex documentation for funding. The absence of an internal team turned out to be a blessing as I got access to many ideas, which past experience shows would not have come internally. Luckily, I was able to get excellent consultants—Gopalan, Rajiv Khaitan and Jessie Paul of Paul Writer. One idea is priceless, and the three of them provided several! Gopalan was there for all financial issues. Rajiv Khaitan is that rare lawyer who steeps himself into the business context beyond the legal formalities. Jessie provided several marketing and branding ideas. I would have also needed specialized help in areas related to people, but luckily Raja Shanmugam, who heads our people practice, sought and obtained an early release. By the time we launched Happiest Minds five months later, we had a lot of foundational blocks in place. All the consultants mentioned here priced their services very reasonably, and I am sure that similarly qualified and affordable consultants are available for start-ups in all major Indian cities.

Creating an advisory board is also something I didn't do at MindTree, but constituted in Happiest Minds. Four global CIOs agreed to come on board. They provided us with many insights and a customer's perspective—that too without any fees. To David Webb of Equifax, Mittu Sridhara of Hepsiburada, Rodney Hefford of Rexam and Steve Peltzman of Forrester, we remain ever grateful.

Another group of external persons you should reach out to for help are mentors, who will also give you very useful advice at no charge. The Indus Entrepreneurs (TiE) and NASSCOM run mentoring programmes and there are scores of successful entrepreneurs who are happy to help young entrepreneurs. In fact, many entrepreneurs have been successful in getting mentor support. Nurturing Green founder Annu Grover has reputedly won mentorship support from as many as four top-notch entrepreneurs: K. Ganesh, Deep Kalra, Rahul Narvekar and Rahul Singh.

Organization Structure

The first thing to know about organization structure is that there is no such thing as the perfect structure in terms of defining individual responsibility. Whatever you decide, there will always be some persons who will criticize it, which is to be expected because all alternative structures have their pros and cons. Secondly, your organization structure defines your go-to-market approach. Any business needs to optimize market access on multiple dimensions such as industry groups, geographical entities or practices. One set of these dimensions will become the main profit centres of the company and the profit centres will then become the power centres of the company. Those centres measured on gross margins and cost will complain that they have an inadequate say in things and are being measured on things they cannot control. For example, in the IT industry we have multiple dimensions to consider in our approach to the customer, including geographical organizations, horizontal domains and vertical industry groups. At Happiest Minds, we had all these dimensions plus another: our business units, which we decided to make our profit centres. These were Digital Transformation and Enterprise Solutions (DT&ES), Infrastructure Maintenance Service and Security (IMSS) and Product Engineering Services (PES). The reason for organizing the company in this fashion is that each of the business heads caters to specific customer groups: the CIO and CMO for DT&ES, the head of Infra or Security for IMSS, and the CTO or head of engineering for PES. This structure has enabled us to understand and speak the language of the customer better. Of course, there were some who thought this structure was not good enough, and truth be told we also saw some of the disadvantages. However, after weighting them out, we consciously decided the BU approach was best for us in our early days. All structures evolve and metamorphose. There is no doubt that as Happiest Minds continues to grow, newer profit centres will emerge and the existing ones may become service lines.

Most people focus on reporting relationships and hierarchy while deciding organization structure. As discussed above, the structure is the vehicle for your go-to-market approach. Accordingly, you should first define your profit centres and then design your reporting structures.

The second aspect to be considered is how the structure can be leveraged to achieve operational efficiency. Finally, the organization structure also has an impact on accountability. For example, at Happiest Minds we decided to wholly integrate our three business units and make them self-sufficient even though it meant duplicating or triplicating some resources. The reason is that we don't want the BUs to have the option of saying they couldn't deliver results because some centralized or corporate department didn't provide operational support in time. Also, things do slow down at organizational boundaries, particularly if you have to rely on a corporate function for people. Integrated structures lead to more agility, operating efficiency and speedy decision-making at a grass-root level.

The conventional wisdom on organization building is to establish a lean, core organization and then invest progressively in people as you earn. This is the right approach for most start-ups. However, if you want to scale rapidly, you will never get there unless you invest upfront. Our principle is that from the very beginning you must build the organization you want to become. For example, at Happiest Minds, we knew our business needed three BUs, multiple industry groups, several global practices, a few geographical heads and six corporate function heads. We put in place senior persons to lead these positions from the start. The majority of the positions were manned by the time we launched the company and the remaining within the next four to five months. Of course, such an approach requires more cash to break even and is only possible if you are sure the requisite cash is committed to the purpose and will be available. You can't implement such an approach with a prayer that a Series B round will come through and when it doesn't, find that you have to dismantle the organization and lay off people. This approach of investing in the structure upfront enabled us at Happiest Minds to become the fastest growing Indian IT services company at a time when the growth of the industry had slowed down from 30 per cent five years earlier to around 10 per cent. The downside of such a high-equity approach is that it will probably depress shareholder returns in the short- and medium-term as compared to a more conservative investment approach. As we are writing this book, we are hoping that a hockey stick effect will eventually kick in after seven years to improve shareholder returns. But even if it doesn't, we believe we had no other option. If you don't scale up rapidly, somebody else will stake the claim to your market.

Talent Acquisition and Talent Retention

The good news is that it's not difficult to attract talent to start-ups. Many young people find the start-up atmosphere exciting and cool. The press conference alone announcing the creation of Happiest Minds brought in 8000-plus applications. As we mentioned, we even found two of our co-founders through the launch announcement. One of them had worked with Ashok earlier but the other one, Prasenjit Saha, Ashok hadn't known at all—though Prasenjit remembers that his appointment letter at Wipro was signed by Ashok just before he left!

Another advantage of a large founding team is that all good leaders have many followers who can bring many of their trusted colleagues along for the ride. So while a large team helps to create a solid foundation, it also helps to diversify your talent base. If not, you will foster subcultures based on where employees have previously worked. Within two years at Happiest Minds, we added talent from over 100 organizations. Still, because we had a significant number of leaders from the two prior organizations Ashok led, some people built perceptions that these close connections were the 'favoured group'. Tackling these prejudices and other negative perceptions goes a long way in talent retention.

In this section on talent, we will not give you any of the dos and don'ts that you can find in most texts on recruitment and selection. Instead, what we would like to share is the learning from mistakes we made in hiring. In Ashok's words:

The first mistake I made was that for the people who worked with me several years before, I did not go through the rigour of a detailed fresh interview. Later, I was surprised that some did not grow as much as I had expected in the intervening years. Also, people change, and you need to be aware of such possibilities. In my MindTree days, I selected as the UK sales head a person who helped build the largest account for Wipro. I was aware of the strong personal relationship he had built with the CIO of the customer organization. With this as proof of performance, I didn't do any reference checks or interview the person in depth. Eight months of zero market development later, we learned that our country head's passion had shifted to horse breeding and a stud farm he had started.

In an increasingly virtual world, some strange things can happen. At an overseas location, we found that a new hire had been able to simultaneously hold a job in a leading IT services company along with ours for over two years before the duplicity was discovered. While this may be an extreme case, it does indicate the need for caution. I am by no means suggesting policing or excessive monitoring. You do need to proceed on the basis of trust, but do put in basic checks as there will always be a few people who will seek to take advantage of the system even in a small start-up.

The opportunity cost of a wrong hire is more than five times the direct cost. Nowhere is this higher than in a sales position. If you have a vacancy and can't find a suitable person to fill it, it is better to ask an existing leader to multiplex and keep you afloat till you get someone who fits the bill. The positions which have the highest mortality rate are field sales positions, probably because sales managers have nowhere to hide when they don't achieve their numbers. I wish I had a few golden rules to share on how to avoid wrong hires of salespeople, but I don't. One thing I do find helpful is that I prefer to hire persons who have had a steady stream of wins even if these are small or mid-size wins. I am wary of persons who boast of only one or two large wins. Odds are that senior sales and business management leaders threw themselves into large deals and took the responsibility for winning. Another aspect for sales positions: order booking times can be large, but it should not delay your time of decision-making for wrong hires. Examine the build-up of the pipeline, both in qualitative and quantitative terms, to come to a conclusion in about six months' time.

While I found talent acquisition surprisingly easy at the start-up stage, the challenges on talent retention begin as you near the three-year period and beyond. The excitement of being in a start-up begins to wear off and the challenges and demands on lifestyle loom larger. A generous ESOP scheme does help retention, but sometimes young people feel wealth monetization through the IPO seems too far away. In this highly competitive talent market, headhunters soon identify your top performers and lure them away with offers of a 50–100 per cent higher compensation, mostly to larger organizations who can afford to pay more. Elsewhere in this book we have covered areas like giving people a sense of purpose beyond their roles and consciously setting out to create a great place to work. One interesting phenomenon I have seen is that business units or departments which are performing well have much lower attrition rates and higher people engagement levels. You could argue that it is the other way around—i.e. higher people engagement and better retention of teams contributes to their better performance. Both statements are true. People like to be part of a winning team and nothing succeeds like success. For high people retention, therefore, it is important to create a continuously reinforcing positive cycle of high performance coupled with great people practices.

KEY TAKEAWAYS

✓ Building your organization begins with creating the right foundation, the responsibility for which rests with the founders.

✓ There are no guidelines to help you ascertain how many founders is right for your venture. But we don't recommend a single founder set-up and VCs also tend to frown upon it.

✓ Most founding teams comprise people who have studied together or worked together. While the bonding helps, too often there is too much similarity in backgrounds. It is important to have complementarity in founder capabilities. If not, there is a tendency to force-fit people into roles.

✓ Our recommended approach is to define the most critical roles which merit being manned by a founder and then choose the right persons to fill those roles. It helps for bonding if some have studied or worked together in the past, but that should not be a criteria for founder selection. If a company in your field has a reputation for excellence in a given area, you will be able to bring in the best practices if you can attract a founder with the relevant experience from that company.

✓ Equity sharing between founders need not be equal or egalitarian, but should be broadly in proportion to expected value addition.

✓ Founders should come in with a salary cut as the start-up won't be able to afford their prior salaries. Even for straight-out-of-college founders, salaries should be below market. The senior-most founders and those who receive the highest equity should take the largest salary cuts. High founder salaries are a red flag for VCs.

✓ Founders have legitimate reason to take pride in being founders, but being a founder is not a role. Neither is it an entitlement to any special concessions. Accordingly, if a founder is not measuring up, he should be treated like any other member of the team: provide maximum support and if things still don't work out, plan for a separation. Since being a founder is a historical fact, it's quite fine to use 'co-founder' as an adjunct to your designation in signatures and visiting cards.

✓ Organization-threatening conflict between founders hits the headlines when it occurs. Fortunately, it is not very frequent. The best way to avoid it is by encouraging debate and a healthy expression of differences in opinion.

✓ Amongst the founders, there must be one who is clearly seen as the 'boss' and whose decision is accepted by all after due debate.

✓ Apart from the founding team, the other entity which plays a key role in foundation building is the statutory board. They are also the guardians for setting the highest standards of corporate governance. Many industry observers are appalled at the poor governance in several start-ups. This can include exaggeration of numbers, negative selling, running down competition and not making a clear distinction between company assets and personal expenditure.

✓ The ideal number of directors for a start-up is three to five persons.

✓ From a corporate governance standpoint, it's best to run your company like a public limited company from its inception. For example, appoint internal auditors even though it's not a statutory requirement for a private limited company.

✓ The most important role in the company is that of the CEO. Though it's a cliché, it's right to say that the buck stops at the CEO and he or she is totally accountable for the annual results.

✓ Most start-ups may think it's far too early to do succession planning for the CEO. But it is in the early stages of a company that excessive dependence on this key individual develops and exigencies or emergencies can happen to any person. Accordingly, one of the key responsibilities of the CEO, in conjunction with the board, is to finalize plans for his or her succession.

✓ Apart from internal auditors, external entities or persons who can help in building your organization are the advisory board, consultants and mentors.

✓ The organization structure is not so much about hierarchies or reporting relationships, but defines your go-to-market approach, operational efficiency and accountability. Organization design should begin with the consideration of these parameters. No organization structure is perfect and structures do need to change from time to time. Your profit centres will determine your organization's power structure. You will need mechanisms to ensure that those who sit on the sidelines of the profit centres don't feel disenfranchised.

✓ The conventional way for building a start-up is to start with a small, core and lean team. As you grow, the investments follow the money. If you want to scale rapidly then you need to create upfront the organization you want to be. The downside of not scaling rapidly is that someone else will occupy the market space you want to own. However, this high-investment approach can only be considered if you have commitment on cash availability. Otherwise, you will expand rapidly only to run out of cash and then come to a grinding halt.

✓ Many young persons today are excited about working in start-ups and find it glamorous. Consequently, attracting talent is not as difficult as most people fear.

✓ The opportunity cost of a wrong hire is five times the direct cost until separation. Thus sometimes it's better for leaders to multiplex and fill the gap than to hire in haste.

✓ The highest opportunity cost is in sales, which also has the highest mortality rates. You need to track lead indicators like pipeline build-up to restrict your opportunity loss on wrong hires.

✓ When you have known someone in the past, you may tend to skip the rigours of a detailed interview and reference checks. This can give you an unpleasant surprise as sometimes people's motivations change, while others' development slows down.

✓ The challenges for talent retention begin as you near the three-year period and the excitement of being in a start-up begins to wear off. Your better people will receive salary offers of 50–100 per cent above their current compensation. Apart from ESOP schemes, what helps is giving people a sense of purpose and consciously creating a great place to work.

✓ People love to be associated with success. Accordingly, the best way to improve people retention is to create a positive, reinforcing cycle of high performance coupled with great people practices.

6.

Business Strategy

'Every battle is won before it's ever fought'

—Sun Tzu

Most books on business strategy present it as one monolithic entity based on time-tested principles of strategy. Ashok has a different take. He sees strategy as a continuum of strategic approaches, which vary considerably during the life cycle and situation of a company. Accordingly, you need a start-up strategy, a scale-up strategy, a strategy to compete against the gorillas in your field, a strategy to pivot if required, a strategy for risk reduction, a strategy to avoid being disrupted by new competition and a strategy for acquisition.

Start-up Strategy

The start-up strategy is the stage where you validate the assumptions and hypotheses that prompted you to adopt the idea you chose to turn into a venture. This includes assumptions on market sizing, including addressable market, competition response to your entry, ease of adoption of your product/service, stickiness and growth potential of your customers and your go-to-market approach. Based on your findings, it is the time to recalibrate your spend budgets.

Many of us like to position our strategies as disruptive. The start-up stage is a good time at which to ask whether your strategies are indeed disruptive. If yes, what kind of disruption are they causing in the market: are you delivering a new genre of product or service, are you delivering an existing service but with a disruptive cost or asset structure (for example, Uber/Ola for car hire), are you disrupting the distribution structure through the elimination of intermediaries, or are you bringing to market new disruptive technologies which can help customers to gain a disruptive advantage in their own businesses? The last assumption was valid for Happiest Minds when we started out. SMAC (social, mobility, analytics, cloud) hadn't become a much-bandied acronym then. Also, we were clear from inception that our strategy would always be SMACPLUS, and we would constantly embrace newer disruptive technologies as they emerged. Accordingly, our technology offerings soon included unified communication, Internet of things (IoT) and AI/cognitive computing.

You also need to be clear if your assumptions on differentiators are valid. At Happiest Minds, our differentiator had to be seen in the context of our competition. While a number of niche mobility- or analytics-only companies had come up, we could truly say that we were the only start-up that could integrate all these technologies into digital transformation solutions. With respect to the older, larger incumbents who claimed to do everything, we could validly state that we were focused and had no baggage to protect.

It's amazing how many new ventures don't proceed beyond the start-up stage to the scale-up stage. The external manifestation is organizational collapse due to the inability to get new funding. The root cause behind lack of subsequent funding is that the original assumptions are no longer valid and course corrections were not done early enough. We won't cite examples as there are literally hundreds strewn over what we sadly call the 'graveyard for new ventures'. It would be fair to add that the maximum number of failures are in the industry which is the flavour of the day—e-commerce for the last few years—as scores of persons rush into this space.

One area of strategy on which Ashok has strong views is price. To quote him: 'Price is not a strategy. It's a mug's game.' It's a pity that so many companies enter the market with the belief that they can create a viable, healthy company by offering discounted prices. If your product or service works on a 30 per cent margin and you give a 10 per cent discount, you have eroded 33.3 per cent of your margin. It's not rocket science to figure that out. Lower pricing is only merited where your costs are lower than the competition and you can sustain your industry-level margins.

In the early days of Happiest Minds, Ashok remembers a large Internet company floating an inquiry for setting up a large offshore development centre. After the usual processing, we were informed that we were selected as one of two successful winners. The other winner was one of the larger Indian IT players. We were told that since we were not even a Tier-2 player yet, we would be given prices 10–20 per cent less than what was offered to the other party. We inquired whether it was because they had a lower expectation on quality or skill profile from our team. The answer was, 'No. The price is lower because you are a Tier-2 vendor.' We didn't appreciate the reasoning and politely declined the opportunity.

Another danger of a low pricing strategy is the negative connotations of being seen as cheap. We believe that the failure of the Nano, the Tata Motors car, is largely due to the declared objective of producing the cheapest-ever car at a price point well below any vehicle in the market. The car had some novel design features and pleasing aesthetics. Tata Motors didn't appreciate that buying a car is an aspirational experience, particularly for someone graduating from a two-wheeler to a four-wheeler. Many such persons didn't want to be seen as having made the cheapest choice. Value for money would have been a far better positioning strategy.

The e-commerce companies have been indulging in huge discounting on the grounds that they are trying to establish an Internet-buying habit. Lower prices can be justified to the extent that e-retailers don't have the brick-and-mortar costs of retailers. E-retailers may have lower costs linked to volume, but if heavy discounting is used to grab market share from each other, then they are only beggaring themselves. A time will come when the large amount of cash raised has been blown away and such discounting is no longer feasible. Our view is that the huge valuations such e-commerce players have been receiving will come crashing down and the existence of at least a few will be threatened.

The exception to the stand against discount pricing is the famous razor/razor-blade pricing strategy. Here, the razor is sold for a cheap price in order to induce the subsequent sales of a 'proprietary' blade. Another example would be original design and manufacturing (ODM) players like Flextronics, Foxcom or Sanmina, who will underprice the design with a view to getting an ongoing manufacturing contract. In both these cases, the pricing for the main product/service has not been compromised. A corollary to the ODM example: if a design services company like MindTree or Happiest Minds finds itself in competition with an ODM, there is no sense in reducing the design price. One strategy is to get the customer to decouple the design and manufacturing contracts. Another possibility is to persuade the winning ODM to buy the design from you. It's more than likely that the design services company will have more focused expertise and will make a decent profit on what it would have cost the ODM to do itself.

Another aspect of start-up strategy is to examine where you are in the value chain of your industry. Most companies work their way up the value chain as the lower ends get increasingly commoditized. Therefore, it's good to find a spot in the value chain which offers you an entry opportunity with better margins. As the market is generally largest at the base of the value chain, a midway point should give you a large enough market at a decent price/margin.

Scale-up Strategy

After you win the start-up challenges, then comes the scale-up battle. Depending on where you started out in the value chain, you have the option of moving up or down to encompass a larger part of the entire chain. Paradoxically, it is more difficult to move down the value chain than to move up. The latter entails acquiring higher value-add skills and is thereby aspirational. Moving down the value chain creates negative vibes in an organization. For example, neither at Happiest Minds nor at MindTree could we have moved into the business process outsourcing (BPO) segment as it would have been seen as incongruent with the DNA of a company operating in a higher value-add space.

Another way of scaling up your business is to enlarge your addressable market by entering new or adjacent market segments. This is the time when you will be faced with the dilemma of 'focus' and depth versus additional breadth. Michael Porter has famously said that strategy is about 'what not to do'. If you can scale by sticking to one or two focus areas, it will be better from a profitability angle and also from the point of view of obtaining leadership in your chosen segment. Mu Sigma, as a focused, analytics-only company (though positioned by Dhiraj Rajaram as a problem-solving company), is an excellent example. On the other hand, focus can also be a double-edged sword. What happens if the chosen market dries up?

When Ashok's co-founders at MindTree chanced upon him through Walden, their business plan was focused only on the Internet. Ashok made only three changes, one of which was to introduce product engineering, in which he and the other team members had considerable experience. When the dot-com bust came without notice, it was the engineering revenue which saw MindTree through till it developed new capabilities.

OneAssist, a company which provides 'protection and peace of mind', has effectively chosen the route of market expansion through additional segments. Gagan Maini, promoter and co-founder, had previously worked in another company in the 'assistance' business. He found that most of the international competition in the industry focused on one product for a single industry. After establishing the concept for OneAssist in the start-up year, he expanded the company's offerings to include two product categories and three industry groups. He also expanded their coverage from things you carry (for example, a mobile phone, a wallet) to things you leave behind at home. Such expanded coverage was consistent with the OneAssist brand and also enlarged sales exponentially through the cross-selling of services.

As you scale your organization, you will increasingly realize that you can't do everything yourself. You probably began some business partnerships on either the sell side or buy side in your start-up phase. In the scale-up phase, partnerships will acquire an even greater importance. Partnerships can be of multiple shades and hues. Most are asymmetric in the sense that one partner is much larger than the other. As a start-up, odds are you will be the smaller party. Try to ensure reciprocity in the agreement, and if you must agree to exclusivity, insist that it is retained only if specified revenue goals are achieved. Intellectual property (IP) is another area which lends itself to partnerships. If you have developed an IP which is of interest to a larger player with much larger market access, you should be open to offering 'white label' access to the player. Likewise, there are many exciting product companies developing new technologies that have limited capability to market their offerings. You should look out for such opportunities and gain access to these IPs on a 'white label' basis. Partnerships with companies which have upstream or downstream capabilities lend themselves very well to joint go-to-market approaches. For example, Happiest Minds has excellent capabilities in designing and deploying digital transformation solutions. So when a global consulting company in the same space agreed to a partnership, we were delighted. Virtually every digital transformation consulting contract leads to identifying road maps for future solutions and afterwards, the consulting company was invited often to be involved in the implementation. Accordingly, they also needed a solutions partner like Happiest Minds for a joint go-to-market with more end-to-end offerings. Many such consulting companies are wary of partnerships with large solutions players as they suspect that sooner or later, the large solutions player will want to eat their lunch. Thus your 'smallness' is an advantage. In our case, it led to a wonderful complementary partnership for Happiest Minds.

The approaches for scaling up can be very different for B2B and B2C companies and some of these key distinctions are appropriately covered in the next chapter on marketing. Several others, where the scaling up requires strategic decisions, are covered here.

First, you should take advantage of today's technologies to 'platformize' your offerings and expand your market reach significantly. The word 'platform', in context of the digital economy, is a hardware/software combination which links buyers and sellers, facilitates external transactions and enables products to be delivered as a service. Uber and Amazon are examples of companies which run on platforms and are also marketplaces provided by e-commerce companies. Platforms can lead to rapid growth and give you streams of revenues in annuity. Platforms play an equally important role in both B2B and B2C businesses. Another very innovative example of platforms is Aadhar. Aadhar could just have been a huge database of residents in India. Instead, Nandan Nilekani created it as a platform with open extensions on the basis of which many ventures could create new business or government applications.

In B2B businesses, apart from platforms there can be many other avenues for annuity business streams such as multi-year contracts, which provide predictable revenues and reduce the cost of selling. For B2C businesses, a great option is when you can make money while you sleep, for example, Facebook or YouTube, which are the biggest content companies and yet own no content—the content is provided free of cost by the consumer.

Equity-linked deals associated with revenue achievement goals can be another area for B2B business growth, but these need to be carefully defined to avoid parting with excess equity. In the IT services industry in India, such arrangements first appeared when GE introduced equity-linked deals as a feature of their three-year contracts, which gave the Indian offshoring players hundreds of millions of dollars per annum. The industry was growing rapidly and the market cap of the leaders reflected this growth. The net effect is that GE must have recovered, through capital gains, a significant proportion of payments made for the work done.

Ashok remembers that in his MindTree days the company did one equity-linked deal with AIG, the world's largest insurance company at the time. The intent was to get a $20 million customer in a finite period, based on the theory that one large customer leads to another. Accordingly, MindTree capped the equity payout to revenue in year three of the business. Fortunately for them, AIG was slow off the block and in year three, billing to AIG had reached only $5–8 million and MindTree parted with only a small fraction of the equity they would have otherwise given. In the next two years the account grew to $20 million, but by then the equity earned had been capped at the year three revenue-linked level! AIG's business continued to grow and was MindTree's largest account for several years. Several other $20 million-plus accounts followed, justifying the primary assumption for the deal.

While talking of scaling up, it's important to note that growth should not be so rapid that it spins out of control. An excellent example of unsustainable growth was Deccan Aviation, whose exponential growth was also accompanied by delayed flights, lost baggage and chaos in general. Fortunately for Captain Gopinath, he was able to find a buyer in Vijay Mallya's Kingfisher Airlines. As usually happens in such cases, the only one who went laughing to the bank was the seller!

Moreover, when we think of scaling up, we mostly think of revenue. But scaling up must include systems, organizational capability and most of all, profitability as well. Revenue growth without adequate profit growth is an exercise in vanity to feed the ego.

The importance of maintaining or increasing profitability while scaling up can be seen in the comparison of Amazon and Alibaba's sales, profits and valuation. The data in the table on the next page is for the quarter ended September 2014, when Alibaba went public.

	Amazon	Alibaba
Revenue ($ billion)	20.8	2.7
Profit /(Loss) ($ million)	(437)	494
Market Valuation ($ billion)	153.1	231.4

Alibaba, a much smaller and younger company than Amazon, managed to get a higher valuation than the industry leader, simply because of its profitability.

Ashok would like to conclude this section with a story about a feedback session with Azim Premji, his chairman at Wipro:

> Wipro's computer business was growing at breakneck speed. We had already overtaken half a dozen computer companies in revenue and I was in a hurry to overtake the only company ahead, HCL, and become number one (which, eventually, we did achieve). During the appraisal session, Premji chided me that another one of his CEOs would have delivered 1 to 2 per cent more of PAT/sales. While conceding this was likely, I responded that if I handled the other CEO's business, I would have grown it by 50 per cent more than its current level. Though Premji didn't quite say touché, he allowed himself a hearty laugh. In any case he too had made his point on profitability. In hindsight, I appreciated the need to be reminded of profitability when we were getting carried away by our huge growth.

Competing against Gorillas

As an entrepreneur, sooner or later you will find yourself competing against the global giants in your industry. This may even happen right at the beginning when you first enter an industry. In other cases, your success itself invites the global leaders to enter a market which you have helped to create. MindTree and Happiest Minds can both be classified in the first category: start-ups entering into a multibillion dollar industry where we had to compete against not only the Indian IT services giants, but also global leaders like IBM, Accenture, Cap Gemini and others. E-commerce players like Flipkart and Snapdeal come in the second category. Their success in creating a large e-commerce market attracted the global leader, Amazon, into India. Another example is Café Coffee Day, whose success in creating a coffee-drinking culture in a nice ambience has drawn Starbucks to India. We will later revisit which of these companies is better equipped to meet this new challenge of a global leader entering your market: Flipkart/Snapdeal or Café Coffee Day.

When you think of competing against giants, the first metaphor which comes to mind is judo strategy. The birth of this strategy lies in the seminal article by C.K. Prahalad and Gary Hamel in *Harvard Business Review*, where they write, 'Competitive innovation is like judo; upset your rivals by using their size against them.' Since then, the principle has been articulated in books like *Judo Strategy* by David Yoffie and Mary Kwak, and also *David and Goliath* by Malcolm Gladwell.

The title story in Gladwell's book brings out the principle of changing the rules of the game, which is what David did. It also highlights the need to exploit the weaknesses of the larger player and shows how to convert the opponent's advantages into disadvantages. The David Yoffie book takes some of the principles of judo discipline and illustrates through examples how to use these in a business context. Even prior to these books, Peter Drucker had used the phrase 'entrepreneurial judo' in his book, *Innovation and Entrepreneurship*. According to Drucker, of all the strategies available to start-ups, entrepreneurial judo is by all odds the least risky and most likely to succeed. He points out that as companies grow, they have a tendency to become all things to all people. They burden their products with feature after feature to cater to every segment. A new entrant can choose one (large) segment and develop a competitive product, which doesn't have a single additional feature beyond what is needed for his or her entry segment of choice. Another approach suggested by Drucker is to secure a beachhead which established leaders don't care to defend and from there make further advances. This principle is exactly what the Indian IT services industry used for disruption and developing what today is a $150 billion industry. The export business began as an offshore mainframe support business. The incumbents didn't want to disturb their business models for a small sliver of the total market. They hardly noticed that the Indian IT industry was moving rapidly from segment to segment. It wasn't until a $20 billion industry had been created that they realized the serious threat. Their response was also to embrace offshoring, which became the default model. Fortunately, even as this cost advantage eroded, the Indian industry had been given time to establish a reputation for process quality and delivering value, ensuring its continued increase in market share.

While judo strategy has become a familiar metaphor for tackling the mighty, Ashok would like to introduce a metaphor based on another ancient discipline, which he labels 'Tai Chi thinking'. In his own words Ashok explains:

Shortly after starting Happiest Minds, we decided to introduce Tai Chi as a part of our wellness programme. We invited Seefar Wellness to present their offerings to us. Seefar is led by Avinash Subramanyam (Avi), who is the leading practitioner of Tai Chi in India. Addressed as sensei (teacher) by his team, he has recently been conferred the title of *soke* by a global body which authorizes him to develop his own systems and moves in martial arts. In the discussion and demo for the Happiest Minds team, Avi brought along his senior trainer, Priya Crasta, all of 5 feet 2 inches, weighing in at 52 kg. As part of their demo, the tallest and strongest amongst our team was invited to push Priya. Try as he might with all his weight, he couldn't budge her an inch. She then asked our team member if she could push him. With less than a flick of a movement, she had him staggering backwards. It had all the drama of a trick by a skilled magician, except that there were no props and it all happened at close quarters, in plain sight. We decided to engage Seefar and I also retained them for personal training at my residence for two days a week, which continues to this day. I inquired from Avi if we could extract some principles from the way Priya had dislodged a much larger 'opponent' that would be of value to entrepreneurs competing against larger players. From our dialogue emerged what I call 'Tai Chi thinking'.

Tai Chi is principally about balancing the yin and yang, which leads to strength in softness. Yin is feminine, passive, absorbent energy, whereas yang is more masculine, aggressive and active energy. The practice of Tai Chi is like a tree which combines flexibility (as it moves with the wind) with the strength which is derived from the nourishment of the root. In Tai Chi, you not only use your opponent's power as is done in judo but absorb it within yourself. When the opponent is strong you yield, indicating no head-on confrontation or bruising battles. Another characteristic of Tai Chi is the ability to move instantaneously from soft to hard and vice versa, and also to sense the opponent's weakness through vibrations, which gives you the ability to know when to strike. The micro movements of Tai Chi also enable you to examine yourself critically and assess your own weaknesses.

Tai Chi is also described as 'meditation in motion', which has benefits similar to the benefits from other meditation forms.

I have, of course, restricted my explanation of Tai Chi thinking to only those principles which an entrepreneur can apply.

Let's go back to the four examples we mentioned at the beginning of this section and see how they fared or are likely to fare in the face of gorilla competition.

In the early years of MindTree and Happiest Minds, we noticed a common phenomenon. We were not invited to the large parties, but whenever we were at the table, competing against the largest players, we won more often than not. In Malcolm Gladwell's book *David and Goliath*, he mentions a study by Ivan Arreguin-Toft stating that in wars between stronger and weaker parties, where the latter used guerilla or unconventional tactics, the weaker party's win percentage was 63.6 per cent! It's not surprising then that both at MindTree and Happiest Minds, we won more than we lost in competitive situations. Some guerrilla tactics we resorted to include offering to do a proof of concept or deliver a prototype before embarking on the whole project. This also shows that all large players have their weaknesses and these can be exploited.

Let's look at a couple of examples. When Aadhar floated an inquiry for the engine to run the world's second largest database, over twenty large players across the globe responded. For the AIG equity deal, six large players were in the initial fray. The winner in both cases: MindTree. A few years later, a multibillion-dollar retailer in the US needed to do a rushed development of an application for an Apple trade show. Four of the largest IT players were already partners doing big business with them. Happiest Minds was not even a listed partner. And yet, we went on to win the deal. A few years later the same retailer became our largest customer. The tactics used in winning these deals included many of the principles of judo strategy and Tai Chi thinking: flexibility, innovation and best-of-breed partnerships to offset the opponents generalized offerings. The retail example above is a good illustration of Tai Chi thinking. We displayed flexibility in our team profile and expressed commitment to meeting the very tight project competition schedule. We were rigid (like the tree trunk) on pricing—we displayed confidence in our ability to provide superior value and were firm that we would not offer a lower price to enter the account. Also, a big disadvantage which we sensed was that large companies are under market pressure to create the equivalent of a mid-sized company annually. For example, a $10 billion company expected to grow at 15 per cent annually has to create $150 million of new business, equivalent to a mid-sized company, every year. Accordingly, they don't have their hearts in winning deals, which often begin as small prototype projects and have a high input (effort) to output (revenue) ratio.

Let's now come to more recent, ongoing and highly visible battles: e-commerce players like Flipkart and Snapdeal versus Amazon, and Café Coffee Day versus Starbucks. We feel that Café Coffee Day is far better equipped to face the challenge of taking on their industry giant than the e-commerce players. The latter have used discounting as a price growth strategy. The result is that they have heavy accumulated losses and depleting cash positions. Lo and behold, Amazon steps in with deep pockets, a wider range of offerings and the ability to out-discount them any day. Notwithstanding this, Flipkart in particular has held on quite well until now, but are they (and the others too) running out of ammunition?

In contrast, take Café Coffee Day. They have built up a network of 1500 stores, plus many thousands of franchised delivery points and serve 1.5 billion cups of tea and coffee per year. Though CCD pricing offers it reasonable margins, it is seen as a value-for-money offering while Starbucks has come in with its premium pricing model like elsewhere in the world—to the exclusion of the mass-volume market in India, a very price-sensitive country. Also, Café Coffee Day has just been able to complete its IPO, raising Rs 1150 crore (about $170 million) to shore up its defences for the future challenge of remaining the market leader.

Finally, another point of difference is between industries which rely on a digital footprint rather than a physical one. The former allows quick entry and expansion at start-up, but is easily replicated by new competition. A physical footprint takes time to build and earlier entrants have a big cost advantage as infrastructure costs keep increasing over time. This may not be a sustainable advantage for, say, banks, who have built up a vast network of physical branches and now face competition from digital players. The new banking players can convert the incumbent's branch assets into a liability (a David and Goliath strategy). On the other hand, for someone whose business is serving millions of cups of coffee every day, the physical infrastructure creates an impregnable defence.

Pivoting Strategy

VCs inform us that many ventures often abandon their original business plan and move into a completely different direction from where they started out. When it becomes clear that the original value proposition is not going to work, it is important to adopt a new value idea, which is still linked to or derived from the original business. This is what is commonly labelled in entrepreneurial parlance as pivoting. Careful thought is needed to decide on whether to persevere or to pivot. Also, you have to be on the lookout for early warning signals. If you must pivot, do so before it's too late. Emotions should not be allowed to enter into the equation as the founders are often passionate and possessive about the original idea.

At MindTree, we set out to be an Internet systems integrator. While the dot-com boom lasted, it was an exciting and fun ride. We were competing against Cambridge Technology Partners, Scient, Viant, Sapient et al. Our pricing was about 30–50 per cent higher than the large Indian IT services players. Heady stuff—and then it all came to an abrupt halt. Ashok told his senior colleagues that they had to develop capabilities like enterprise resource planning (ERP), data warehousing and even a mainframe practice to survive, all of which would make MindTree look like any other player. As the large players had so much more experience and many use cases in these segments, there was legitimate concern on why any customer would choose to come to MindTree for these same services. There was almost a feeling of betrayal in the minds of some of the co-founders who expressed that this is not what they had set out to do. Yet, they all realized that the original business had dried up and there was no other option for survival. Thus, MindTree began its pivoting journey. The next two years seemed to confirm the doubts of the naysayers. MindTree was barely adding $2–3 million in revenue each year, but despite this Ashok was confident that they were adding new capabilities which would eventually show results. Different approaches were adopted for different areas. They were struggling to grow the ERP practice. Volvo, for whom they were an exclusive partner in the Internet space, was seriously considering other partners for its ERP needs. Then,

MindTree went out and acquired an eighty-person-strong ERP company in Delhi to supplement its own forty-person team and managed to save the account. Other ERP customers followed. For mainframes, the equity deal with AIG gave them an anchor client and drove the segment's growth. In data warehousing and remote infrastructure management (RIM), both underserved and underpenetrated areas, they were able to build organically. Three years into the pivoting strategy, things began to pick up. In the fourth year after pivoting (the sixth year from inception), the combined efforts bore fruit and MindTree grew from $55 million to $100 million to become the fastest Indian IT services company to reach $100 million in sales.

All pivoting stories don't work out as well. Sometimes three or even four pivots are needed. This can only happen when the VCs retain confidence and faith in the team.

Deepak Kamra, a Silicon Valley-based VC who is sometimes known as the 'love value chain investor' (because he has led investments in the world's most popular dating site, Match.com, the world's largest matrimonial services site, Bharat Matrimony and the world's largest dating application, Zoosh.com), shares one pivoting example. In 1995, Match.com pitched itself to Canaan as a platform for 'classifieds', with the assumption that classifieds would move to the Internet. It was agreed with the founders that the concept must first be proved in one segment, and so they started with dating. It so happened that the vertical turned out to be more exciting. What could have been a technology play that would have become rapidly commoditized ended up as a first-of-its-kind e-commerce play.

Eric Ries, in his book *The Lean Startup*, identifies, amongst others, the following types of pivots:

- A zoom-in pivot, where a feature becomes the whole product

- A zoom-out pivot, the reverse of the above
- A customer segment pivot, where the product is okay but better meets the need of another market
- A customer need pivot, which sometimes requires a completely new product
- A platform pivot, which involves change from an application to a platform or vice versa
- A business architecture pivot, which may even involve changing B2B into B2C or vice versa

An article in the *Economic Times* of 22 May 2016 by Rajiv Singh provocatively raises the issue whether 'pivoting might have just become the new fig leaf for failure'. Some of the entrepreneurs featured express the fear that pivoting is being used as a ploy to raise additional money. Not surprisingly, the entrepreneurs featured in this article who have done multiple pivots defend their pivoting decisions. The same article lists some of the most successful pivots globally, which, as per them, include YouTube, PayPal, Flickr and Twitter. These examples alone prove that there are many situations where pivots are not only justified, but a strategic imperative.

Adopting a pivoting strategy requires a lot of serious thought. All the disciplines on idea validation given in the first chapter need to be deployed here. The team needs to be aligned behind the new approach. Once the decision is taken, you need to move full steam ahead.

Risk Minimization Strategy

All business is about risk and all decision-makers, be they entrepreneurs or otherwise, are risk-takers. It comes with the territory. We are puzzled when entrepreneurs exclusively are characterized as being risk-takers. This creates a macho image of an entrepreneur and the sense of bravado it lends can lead to excessive, sometimes unnecessary risk-taking. Our view is that the job of all entrepreneurs is risk minimization, while being cognizant of the fact that all strategy decisions involve some risk.

In this section, we are not going to talk about the kind of risks listed in IPO documents or things like compliance risks, talent risks, security risks or fraud risks, which any company must have programmes, processes and checks and balances to guard against. We are also not talking about risks which occur due to external events which you cannot control. In an increasingly uncertain world you can hardly predict where and when such events might occur. Who, for example, could have predicted 9/11, the post-Lehman Wall Street crash or that a dramatic drop would take place in oil prices so soon after their crazy rise? As someone succinctly put it, all you can predict is a high probability of one of several low-probability events occurring every four to five years (or less) which will impact your business. The simplest and in our view the most effective approach is to classify all risks into two categories: those that have a dramatic impact on your revenue and those that significantly increase your cost structure. For each category, draw up a list of possible actions. When the external event does occur, validate and fine-tune the action plan—and move with haste.

Our approach in this section is to focus on the risks which occur due to strategic decisions. We can further classify these as the 'sins of omission and commission'. Those in the first category are more difficult to anticipate because we don't know what we don't know. Changes are taking place in the world at an ever-increasing pace. Today's disruptor can be tomorrow's disruptee (apologies as the word doesn't exist in the English dictionary, but we trust you get the meaning). The most common cause of the sins of omission is not realizing how technology breakthroughs can change the business model and also missing out when competition emerges from new sources and different industries.

In an article titled 'How Banks Can Stave off the Challenge from Technology Companies?' by Sneha Jha (*Economic Times*, 15 December 2015), Uday Kotak, one of India's most successful banking industry entrepreneurs, is quoted as saying: 'I am very challenged. I keep wondering at night, will I have a bank the next morning, or will some technology company be doing banking without needing a bank?' It is paranoia of this type which is needed to avoid the sins of omission. Seeing the changes transpiring in the banking industry, you could say that Uday's paranoia is justified. Similar disruptions are taking place in many other industries. And yet, leaders who set out to disrupt businesses miss these changes and get disrupted themselves. The solution? Probably a two-part approach: one of creating a group to continuously scan the horizon for such changes, and if the need is felt, to engage industry-focused consultants whose job it is to predict and monitor such changes. More important, though, is the mindset of top management to take time away from running the business to review and socialize the impact of such changes.

The second category of sins of commission are, as we said, easier to identify. One principle here is to course correct and abort the decision before it assumes proportions that can seriously hurt the company or even threaten its existence. As an example, Ashok would like to talk about a heavily criticized decision for which he was responsible:

> In 2010, a couple of years after MindTree's IPO, an opportunity was brought to us for acquiring Kyocera's captive development centre. The centre, incidentally, was located adjacent to our main development centre in the

picturesque Global Village, Bangalore. This captive centre used to design phones for Kyocera's phone business and also undertake engineering work for other Kyocera projects. We saw this as a good complement to our own communications engineering capability with the potential to open up a new customer base. The company had excellent equipment and labs, and there was also scope to get $20 million of design services revenue from Kyocera over the next three years. We put in a successful bid of $5.5 million. If we had stopped there, it would have been an extremely low-risk acquisition paying for itself over just two years of service revenues.

But even while the talks were going on, the local Kyocera team which we were to acquire presented to us the phones they had designed. These were impressive. They also presented to us an interesting design idea for a smartphone which focused on the needs of the social media generation. Samartha Nagabhushanam, the CEO of Kyocera India, suggested that we needn't restrict ourselves to design services and could design complete phones, but no longer for one in-house buyer. We discussed that the phone could be supplied on an OEM basis to large telecom companies under their brand, with manufacturing outsourced to China except for final testing and quality assurance for which the captive centre already had the equipment. My impression was that by avoiding investments in brand building, distribution and manufacturing, we had sufficiently de-risked the project. Accordingly, we decided to put forth the proposal to the board. Though we had a high-powered board (including one member who had studied the business of two leading global phone manufacturers), the approval came through without a single note of dissent. It was possible that they had observed that I was personally enthused about the project—at times there is danger of having a successful track record insofar as others always go along with your recommendations. The only member to express concern was Lip-Bu Tan, who by then was no longer on our board. By the time I met him in the US, the die was already cast.

In about six months we already had a working phone design. One of the world's leading telecom companies expressed prima facie interest and began testing the product. In tandem we were given a draft contract. It was only then that we realized that we knew all about designing a phone, but didn't know anything about marketing it. By supplying the phones on an OEM basis, we thought we were also avoiding an inventory risk as supplies would be against firm orders. The contract we received was extremely one-sided. One clause, for example, required us to take back any unsold inventory. In an industry where prices decline sharply, what would we have done with sales returns of a private labelled product? A few of my senior colleagues began clamouring for closure. I waited another six weeks till the test report from the telecom major came to us. They liked the product but wanted two design changes. I concluded that the additional design effort was not worth it and the project was too risky. So I put up a closure proposal to the board, which they accepted as quickly as they had approved the proposal!

We lost about $8 million in the misadventure which was offset by the margins we made on the service revenue over the next few years. Of course, we could have got the service revenue without blowing up $8 million! By then MindTree was generating about $50 million of cash every year. We stopped well before we bet the company, but the amount we lost that year was significant and severely impacted the share price of the company. Even if the financials had been better, I later realized that the project was doomed to fail, for reasons I will discuss in the next section on acquisition strategy.

Looking back on our decision-making, I reflect on how the decision went through with so little challenge, pushback or dissent. Understanding this, I felt, was more important from the angle of the future rather than whether the decision was right or wrong. The following thoughts came to my mind:

- First, the process of project endorsement was inverted. Normally, a business unit (BU) or an industry group (IG) or the M & A team would put up proposals that required strategic decision-making. Many non-viable ideas got weeded out at that level and only a few reached my desk. Here, the proposal for the acquisition came to me through a BU, but the idea for designing/manufacturing phones for the market was sold in parallel by the Kyocera team to the BU head and myself. Both of us had a manufacturing background and in a way, the phone project was like returning to our roots.

- I abandoned my own head, heart and gut in the decision-making process and indicated my interest too quickly in the project.

- Our internal board comprised three other persons apart from myself. Of them, two had begun their careers with me at Wipro, from campus selection onwards. They seldom disagreed with me or voiced their concerns, possibly because I had guided them through their career growth and because of my track record of success. This implicit endorsement added to my own sense of hubris as I had had no major failures in my career till then. Apart from the internal board members, our statutory board comprised two VCs, who were wonderfully supportive, but like my two colleagues mentioned earlier were also inclined to say 'whatever you decide is fine'. The external board members were truly high profile. Two of them had a manufacturing background and one understood the global phone business exceedingly well. Along with the others, they probably saw the market size and also shared the view that if anyone from India could succeed in making a phone, it was our team leading the Kyocera team.

What would I do differently for the future?

- I would ensure that I don't get into the decision-making process too early and instead, be the one to challenge the recommendation—which is my role—rather than convey an implicit endorsement.
- If I sense that there has been too much 'group think' even within the board, I will create a team of devil's advocates. Even if this doesn't lead to a change in the decision, the action will throw up potential risks and will enable the drawing up of risk mitigation strategies in advance.

Acquisition Strategy

As a part of your growth strategy, you will sooner or later want to move towards acquisitions. However, an acquisition should not just be manoeuvred for scaling up. You need to be clear on what strategic objectives the acquisition helps to attain. These can include:

- Access to new, marquee customers
- Access to new market segments or geographies
- Critical mass or leadership in an offering or segment
- New domain knowledge—can be vertical or horizontal
- Acquiring intellectual property
- A defensive strategy to protect your base, like the ERP company acquisition by MindTree
- Complementary capabilities

If the target company fulfils several of these objectives, it is a great opportunity.

We would recommend that the acquisition target be in a market which is growing equal to or faster than your company. If not, the acquisition will bring down your growth rate, which you wouldn't want at an early stage of your company's life. The acquisition of Linc, an IBM iSeries focused company, by MindTree, did not fulfil this criteria as it was a slow growth market, but it did provide complementary capabilities. MindTree's IBM practice was only focused on mainframes. The Linc addition made it more complete. Fortunately, MindTree at this stage was growing at 60 per cent per annum and Linc was so much smaller that it hardly made a dent on MindTree's growth rate.

We should also be wary of acquiring loss-making companies. As a start-up, you need to husband and preserve your cash. Also, remember the 'time to next round' decision-making principle articulated earlier.

The Aztecsoft acquisition by MindTree in 2009, shortly after MindTree's IPO, is an example of the ideal acquisition.

Aztecsoft had two business lines—product engineering services (PES) and testing. The Aztec PES business was focused on software and independent software vendors (ISVs). MindTree's PES business specialized in hardware, embedded systems and communications. So Aztec brought in wonderful complementary capabilities. Separately in testing, both companies had a team size of 1000 each but specialization areas were different. Put together, this joint team became a formidable testing force, which at that time was one of the fastest-growing segments for the Indian IT industry.

Also, Aztec had built Microsoft into a $20 million-plus account. Along with MindTree's smaller Microsoft business, this soon became the largest account for MindTree and today, is MindTree's only account which is about $100 million. To top it all, Aztecsoft was a profitable company and yet, MindTree acquired it at a very reasonable price, partly because the world was slowing down before the economic recession hit and the software industry was experiencing its lowest growth rate in many years.

A lot has been written about the reasons for the successes and failures of M & As. Two areas which are often overlooked are business rhythms/models and cultural compatibility. Let's take the case of the Kyocera acquisition by MindTree. The business model for a product business requires high upfront investment with a much higher risk of failure and higher rewards if successful. The IT services business is an instant gratification business. You take up work and get paid month on month on a fairly predictable basis, generating a growing stream of revenue and services. While we'd prefer not to generalize that there is always a big cultural difference between product and service companies, certainly there was a huge difference between Kyocera and MindTree. Select senior members of the Kyocera team saw themselves as a superior breed compared to those in the services sector. This attitude gradually percolated downwards. Since the services business was funding the product investment, much resentment built up in the parent company. Support needed by the erstwhile Kyocera team was held back or given grudgingly. Ashok's attempts to intervene at times (because MindTree had its own investment to protect) was perceived as favouring the new team. As the product development investments led to losses and affected MindTree's results, the share prices went down and the resentment exploded into anger. The lesson for Ashok was that one shouldn't combine businesses with such different rhythms under the same corporate umbrella or try to force-fit disparate cultures. This might be a reason why Infosys has moved its product arm out of the main company (CoreCo) into EdgeVerve (NewCo). As Ashok stated earlier, even if the phone design had been approved, the acquisition could not have succeeded. The cultural mismatch only hastened the decision to put closure to the product project.

One final word of advice on structuring acquisition deals. Think back to the plans you presented to your VCs. They most likely presented ambitious, if not inflated, numbers. Likewise, the target company will make their case for valuation on the basis of ambitious revenue and profit projections. The best way to handle the acquisition is to structure deals with a three-year earn-out with, say, about 40 per cent of the total amount being contingent on meeting the projected numbers.

Let us end on a note of caution. Every strategy is only as good as its implementation. This may seem to be a contradiction of Sun Tzu's statement with which we started the chapter. But, as G.K. Chesterton said, 'All generalizations are untrue, including this one!' Of course, strategy is critical, not just as you get off the block but, as we have seen, right through the life cycle of your company. So is detailed planning and great execution.

Good execution begins by working backwards from the three- or five-year vision. This leads to a roadmap of actions which propel you towards achieving your strategic goals.

KEY TAKEAWAYS

✓ You need a continuum of strategies, including a start-up strategy, a scale-up strategy, a strategy to compete against much larger players, a strategy to pivot if required, a strategy for risk reduction and a strategy for acquisition. For every inflection point in your company or major externally induced change, you need to revisit your business strategy.

✓ In the start-up stage, the key need is to question and validate all the assumptions you made while starting up.

✓ Price is not a strategy; it's a mug's game. Market entry at lower prices is only justified if your costs are lower, allowing you to sustain healthy margins.

✓ The basic dilemma you will face during the scale-up stage is focus versus the addition of new products or services. Focus on one segment, if it is a large market, can help you to get leadership in your chosen area with higher profitability. However, very narrow focus has its own hazards as markets change and your focus area can dry up.

✓ Partnerships become of high importance in the scale-up stage. Since the partner is most likely to be larger, please ensure that this asymmetry doesn't work against you.

✓ Partnerships with companies in upstream or downstream businesses are very likely to be synergistic and offer joint go-to-market approaches by providing more end-to-end solutions.

✓ Intellectual property (IP) offerings lend themselves to partnerships. You can invite larger companies to white label your IPs and, in turn, you can white label IP offerings of other start-ups or small companies. The objective in both cases is to increase market address.

✓ Platformization of your offerings is a great tool to scale both B2B and B2C markets. In B2B, it can yield you annuity business in the form of multi-year contracts. In B2C, it helps you to enlarge your reach and lower your customer acquisition costs. Platforms can help you make money while you sleep.

✓ Equity-linked deals connected to revenue achievement goals are also a way of increasing B2B growth. Deals need to be carefully structured and equity-capped at the revenue achieved in, say, three years. Future revenue increases from the same account don't earn additional equity.

✓ Scaling up should be manageable and not so rapid that it spins out of control.

✓ Scaling up is not just in terms of revenue. It must include systems, organizational capability and most of all, profitability.

✓ For competing against large competition, the first metaphor that comes to mind is judo strategy where you upset your rivals by using their size against them.

✓ Another metaphor is that of Tai Chi thinking. Tai Chi derives strength from softness and moving instantaneously from soft to hard and vice versa. An apt Tai Chi analogy is to be like a tree which combines flexibility as it moves with the wind and the strength it receives from the nourishment of its roots.

✓ Studies show that a small army defeats an army ten times its size 63.6 per cent of the time when it employs guerilla or unconventional tactics. All large companies have their own weaknesses. In each situation, you have to find the large player's weaknesses and develop suitable tactics to take advantage of these. This is borne out of the experience of both MindTree and Happiest Minds, who found that they won more than they lost when they competed against large players.

✓ For competing against a large player entering into your market, physical infrastructure built ahead of time is a better defence than digital infrastructure which the new entrant can quickly replicate or improve.

✓ If it is clear that your original value proposition will not always succeed, you must be ready to pivot. For pivoting, it's necessary to look out for early warning signs so that you can act before it is too late. There are various kinds of 'pivot approaches' and you need to assess which type is the best for you.

✓ All business is about taking risks. It is not sensible to characterize entrepreneurs alone as risk-takers. In fact, the role of an entrepreneur is to be a risk minimizer.

✓ Risks which occur due to strategic decisions can be classified as the 'sins of omission and commission'.

✓ Today's disruptor can be tomorrow's disrupted company. This happens most frequently when you don't notice competition emerging from completely different industries.

✓ Before you take major strategic decisions, see if there has been adequate constructive criticism and debate. If there has been too much 'group think', appoint a 'devil's advocate' team to examine the proposal.

✓ Acquisitions should not just be for scaling up. They should fulfil one or more strategic objectives such as access to new market segments, new geographies, new domain knowledge, acquiring intellectual property, etc.

✓ It is good to look at acquisitions in high-growth markets, so that the acquisition doesn't reduce your own growth rate.

✓ It is better to avoid loss-making companies to conserve your own cash.

✓ Most acquisition failures are due to cultural incompatibility.

✓ It is preferable to structure acquisition deals with an earn-out component spread over two to three years.

✓ Every strategy is only as good as its implementation. Good execution requires working backwards from the three- or five-year vision and drawing up a roadmap of actions.

7.

Marketing Strategy

'Marketing is too important to be left to the marketing department'

—David Packard

I n recent years, few functions have changed so dramatically as marketing, thanks to the advent of digital technologies and social media. David Packard's comment is to be seen in this context. It is not a negative statement on marketing departments, rather a positive summation of how all parts of the company must come together to contribute to the brand story and the role of business leadership in making this happen.

Marketing challenges and approaches differ widely between B2B and B2C companies. (There is also a lesser understood category of B2B2C, which we will discuss later.) But while there are significant differences in marketing amongst these categories, there are also a lot of similarities. As in the previous chapter, we will illustrate our points largely through Ashok's experience of building three B2B businesses (Wipro, MindTree and Happiest Minds) as well as from the best practices of the many B2C customers of these companies. Let us begin with the common principles.

Marketing Principles Common to B2B and B2C Models

- **Building a brand:** One of the basic responsibilities of marketing is to build your company brand and ensure that the actions of the company are consistent with the brand promise. A brand has two major dimensions: the market brand and the supply side brand, the latter which is relevant for attracting and retaining talent. The brand image must be consistent or complementary for both. The brand, like the business strategy, must be aligned with the company's mission, vision and values.

  Branding begins with the company name. As compared to B2B companies, consumer companies generally do a better job at this—think Flipkart, Snapdeal, Amazon, Alibaba, Paytm, among others. Many B2B companies have boring or unexciting names, but the companies have become so powerful that the strength has rubbed off on their brands; examples include IBM, GE, HCL, TCS etc. Both the companies co-founded by Ashok, MindTree and Happiest Minds, have intriguing names which lend themselves to storytelling and increase memorability. MindTree appears in the Upanishads as *mano vriksha* and means a source of eternal intellect for those who come in contact with it, because it springs from the mind. We have already discussed in a previous chapter how the Happiest Minds name is closely aligned with its mission, vision and values. Ashok recollects a discussion with a visiting customer who told his wife that he was going to meet with a company called Happiest Minds later that day. 'How lovely,' she exclaimed. 'I'd love to join.' Would such a conversation ever have taken place if we had been named some add-on to infotech?

- **The best publicity is free publicity:** When a third party says or writes something positive about you or your company, it carries so much more credibility than anything you can say in a paid advertisement. The free publicity you get can include an article by a renowned journalist in a reputed magazine or paper, third-party blogs, references or ratings on social media and, the most powerful of all, customer testimonials. While we have stated that third-party references have much more credibility than your own declarations, even these self-made statements have an important role to play in a content-driven world. You and your team need to project your expertise and capabilities by offering articles for publication to leading business and industry-specific media as well as leading economic and daily newspapers in all the major markets you operate in. LinkedIn has started publishing short articles under the heading 'Pulse', another excellent medium engaging on which gives you global coverage.

To get a vast amount of value through free coverage, you have to be interesting and project yourself as being interesting. Of all the persons Ashok has known, it's Subroto Bagchi who has a knack for deriving the maximum PR value for free. Within a few months of starting MindTree, the company had been featured in the *Wall Street Journal* and the *New York Times*. The former came forward more out of curiosity to learn why a person leading Wipro Technologies would start what seemed to be a niche IT services company. The *New York Times* coverage headlined MindTree as 'a new type of software company from India', with a photograph of Subroto and Ashok in MindTree's development facility. This feature was driven by Subroto's idea of covering the walls of all our facilities with blow-ups of very colourful paintings made by children from the Spastics Society of Karnataka. All internal events were converted into major PR opportunities. For example, MindTree's tenth anniversary led to a series of write-ups on how ten founders had stayed together for ten years. Subroto, also a storyteller and chronicler, wrote many articles including the 'Making of MindTree', which was published in a leading business magazine.

When Happiest Minds began, the theme and message of 'happiness' received immediate attention and we got enormous coverage, leading to brand recognition at a very early stage. As we advanced our IPs and digital transformation solutions, our marketing team (comprising only three persons, led by Salil Godika) did an excellent job of getting these developments featured across a variety of media. Very soon, we had bagged multiple top listings on search engines on our capabilities including retail, analytics, digital transformation and, of course, happiness. These rankings tend to change from time to time so you can never rest on your laurels. The gratifying aspect of all this was that we started receiving multiple business leads through our website, some of which were converted into our largest customers.

Even creating a logo, the visual symbol of your brand, need not be an expensive effort. At MindTree, the logo was designed by inviting children of the Spastics Society to submit their interpretation of the company DNA, 'Imagination, Action and Joy'. The

Happiest Minds logo was a crowdsourced effort with a professional in Cognizant, New Jersey, submitting the winning design.

You may feel that building a brand without much marketing spend is possible only for B2B companies—it is not. As an example of a B2C company which established a brand in the US market, TutorVista stands out for achieving brand recognition with negligible spend. Their target market was the social media-savvy generation and these channels were effectively leveraged.

Customer references are a very powerful source of brand building at no cost. The Happiest Minds marketing department, realizing the importance of this, decided to distribute customer testimonials across the website instead of having these bunched together on a single screen. If these were all together, the first two may be read, but after that the eyes would tend to glaze over the rest. Well-placed testimonials highlighting specific stories can be even more effective than a paid advertisement which pops up as you surf Bing or Google. This is not to devalue the importance of such ads; they are directed straight to the target audience and are also relatively inexpensive.

To conclude, Ashok shares:

In our MindTree days, Subroto never ceased to complain (very vocally) that I approved only paltry marketing budgets within which he had to work. I hope that, looking back, he will appreciate that a tight budget approach brought out the best in his creativity! I would certainly recommend tightening of all marketing budgets even in the

B2C world, where in my view too much money is deployed on spray-and-pray advertising and marketing campaigns.

- **Marketing in a digital world:** We mentioned earlier that no business function has changed as much in recent years as marketing has. We live in a digital world where everybody and everything is interconnected. Concepts such as permission marketing have died a natural death. Instead, we have proximity marketing, predictive marketing, context-aware marketing etc. Marketing has consequently become intrusive because we're always connected and it's important for organizations to wield this new power with care.

  Many of these developments are obviously more important for B2C businesses, but B2B companies will ignore them at their own peril. Happiest Minds is still an emerging company, but in its fourth year, we had over 2000 digital connects, which include analyst connects, CXOs and PR coverage. This does not include visits, page likes and followership on social media sites like Facebook, Google Plus, LinkedIn and Twitter, where the company has a presence which is disproportionately high as compared to its much larger competitors.

- **Building trust:** Building trust with customers is another critically important area common to both B2B and B2C businesses. Of course, the organization has first got to behave in a trustworthy manner and then communicate the message in such a way that 'trust' becomes an important brand attribute strongly associated with your company.

  Ashok asked Bhoomika, an MBA student at the Welingkar Institute of Management Development and Research, which e-commerce site she uses most for online shopping. Her response was that all the sites she has visited are pretty much the same in sending her information on deals, cross-selling options, new offerings etc. However, she prefers to buy from one particular site, Flipkart. On further probing, she replied that it is because she trusts this site the most. It so transpires that most e-commerce businesses get about 99 per cent of their transactions right. It's how you handle the 1 per cent exceptions that makes the difference. Bhoomika's favourite site's advertising focuses on easy returns with no questions asked; her own experience confirms this to be true. Accordingly, trust has built up due to Flipkart's behaviour, which matches the advertisement claim. Another plus of the site's advertising is that they feature people who could be everyday consumers, which gives them much higher credibility than using film stars or cricketers who cost a bomb and who endorse about twenty brands each.

Trust plays an even greater role in B2B relationships, but we will dwell on this further in the section on B2B marketing.

- **Platformization:** As explained in the previous chapter, new digital technologies and low-cost availability of communication bandwidth have made possible what is known as the platformization of your offerings. In the B2B space, platforms enable you to deliver your offerings on a software-as-a-service (SaaS) model, giving you annuity revenue streams; also, the base platform can be customized as per different industry needs. In the B2C space, platforms provide reach and scalability and improve the customer experience.

- **Leverage partner programmes:** Another inexpensive and effective approach to marketing is to leverage the go-to-market programmes of larger partners. Intel organizes industry-wide trade shows in which enterprises that are their customers can get access to the latest solutions from their portfolio companies. Microsoft has an Accelerator programme in which they play matchmaker for many start-ups and enterprises and help is even provided in developing the pitch or tweaking the product in order to leverage programmes of larger partners. Programmes like these address the biggest problem of most start-ups—that of getting access to enterprise customers. Though Happiest Minds has had extensive enterprise relationships, we also benefited greatly from these programmes.

B2C Marketing

The essential difference between B2C marketing and B2B marketing is that the latter addresses a finite number of customers, probably not more than 200 for the first few years after start-up. On the other hand, B2C marketing seeks to reach out to thousands of customers and tries to understand each of them on a personalized basis. The lifetime value of B2B customers is many times higher, while B2C marketing involves shorter sales cycles and many more transactions per customer, but also seeks to establish multi-year relationships through loyalty programmes, promotional coupons etc. These major differences determine the unique approaches taken by B2C marketers towards their customers.

The exciting competition between e-commerce players and traditional brick-and-mortar players is leading to many advances on how to reach, understand and influence the consumer. The name of the game is to be lead adopters in the latest technologies, which give businesses more and more real-time information on their customers, their emotions, the time they spend on their site, what brings them close to making a purchase decision and why they move away. Predictive analytics, algorithms and big data analysis are all involved. The latest technology frontiers being exploited are the Internet of things (IoT), artificial intelligence (AI) and machine-to-machine learning.

Omnichannel capability is increasingly deployed to reach customers. That's why, when a leading e-commerce site recently declared a mobility-only strategy, it puzzled us. There will always be consumers, like us, who prefer to do our transactions on laptops or tablets. Why discard one channel which gives the consumer access, presumably because of the incremental cost of supporting a second platform?

At Happiest Minds, we have found that as brick-and-mortar retailers fight back against e-commerce players, they are taking the lead in exploiting the power of digital technologies and omnichannel platforms. Happiest Minds customers like Sears, Lowe's and Kohl's successfully deploy omnichannel solutions to enhance the in-store customer experience with location-enabled services, personalization for getting insights and stimulating customer engagement.

Jessie Paul, the founder of a marketing consulting company, has handled a number of assignments for Happiest Minds even when we were starting up. We asked her, as we did with Bhoomika, which women's shopping site she felt did the best marketing. There was only one common name on both their lists which, therefore, deserves special mention: LimeRoad. It is more a social than a shopping platform, which ensures high engagement and repeat business and is supported by a tight supply chain. The beauty is that their scrapbook platform, in which customers can curate lookbooks, works like a crowdsourcing forum that generates community-led content. Most other brands pay for this structure, which brings us back to one of our earlier points that the best marketing is free.

An important success factor for B2C companies is the ability to scale. Bangalore-based Qwikcilver, a gift card solutions provider, has quickly scaled to managing 12 million transactions a year through a highly secured platform which provides unique real-time, multi-country, multi-currency capabilities. It is no wonder it has attracted repeat investments from its original investors, Helion and Accel, and the second round was led by Amazon.

An area where B2C companies often trip up is in offering too much choice, particularly in pricing schemes. This confuses the customer and delays his or her purchasing decision. In this respect, TutorVista's buffet pricing model of $100 a month was a brilliant approach in terms of simplicity. An excellent guide for B2C marketing regarding how much choice to provide is Sheena Iyengar's *The Art of Choosing*.

The B2B2C Model

The B2B2C model can be of two types: one is in which businesses sell through e-commerce portals, and the other in which a business whose target is the end consumer sells through a corporate entity. Here, the provider of the product or service is using the intermediate entity as a channel and also an aggregator of demand. Many of the success factors are similar to B2B sales, which we will discuss shortly. For the service provider, the B2B2C model has the advantage of reducing the cost of sales as a single contract with the intermediate entity is adequate to reach hundreds or even thousands of consumers. It also enables the provider to leverage the affinity relationships of the 'B' at the centre. Simultaneously, the service provider has to ensure engagement with each individual consumer such that his or her expectations have to be fulfilled. In this respect, the B2B2C structure is like a B2C sale and also needs a scalable engagement platform. An excellent example of a B2B2C model is OneAssist, which has been able to win thousands of customers in four years and has successfully completed a series B round led by Assurant Solutions along with first-round investors, Sequoia and Lightspeed. Many B2B2C companies also introduce direct B2C sales after establishing a base. Gagan Maini, co-founder and director at OneAssist, told us this would be his next step, and over five years, he expects to achieve 50 per cent of sales directly from the B2C route.

B2B Marketing

Ashok has had many years of experience in B2B, starting from the days he sold hermetic compressors for Shriram Refrigeration, followed by selling minicomputers at Wipro and the rich experience of enterprise solutions sales at Wipro, MindTree and Happiest Minds. He has seen the B2B model evolve over time, but one thing hasn't changed: the most important ingredient for a successful and sustained B2B relationship is trust. Also still the same: the anxiety the business experiences till you win your first few customers who are really, really precious and special for you, and what helps most in getting such customers is having built trust-based relationships. A useful website to look at in this context is FirstFewCustomers.com. The content here is user generated as entrepreneurs share how they won their first few customers and it's possible that some of their experiences may provide important teachings for you.

Ashok narrates how trust played a role in winning the first few customers at Happiest Minds:

When we began both MindTree and Happiest Minds, my biggest worry was: why should anyone give us business when he or she has a choice of over 150 IT service companies, including many multibillion dollar entities? The earliest calls to customers we knew and had developed from scratch seemed to confirm these fears. The typical response was: we know we entered this account because of you (or some other member in your new team), but we already have too many partners and want to consolidate rather than add to them. The trust aspect manifested when the CTO of TomTom, Aref Matin, moved into a new company, WAC, around the time that Happiest Minds was being launched, and Mittu Sridhara, CIO of Ladbrokes, moved into TUI. Both of them had been customers of my prior company and both had a choice. It was particularly gratifying when they chose us.

In Aref's case, the prime factor was the team led by my colleague, Nanda. They had executed operations flawlessly for him across multiple relationships and he swore by the team. It also helped that Aref and I had developed a great deal of mutual trust and respect. Aref became Happiest Minds' first customer at WAC, which was an open, global alliance made up of the world's largest phone manufacturers and networks. Many operators had to be boarded on to the platform, and under Aref's guidance we delivered multiple successful implementations. Aref saw the disruptive changes technology was creating in education and he joined the edutech space, where he helped us in developing two different accounts, including one that became our largest customer. He still continues as a customer at Ascend, a rapidly growing edutech company.

Mittu brought us into Ladbrokes and became our first customer in the UK. Later, as he moved into new assignments he also took us to two new customers. My perception is that Mittu chose us in preference to other prior partners as he had trust that if things ever went wrong, we would deal with them thoroughly and go the extra mile to solve the problem. Mittu has since taken Happiest Minds into a completely new country, where he is our customer in Hepsiburada, Turkey's largest e-commerce company.

Over the years, I can think of five more customers who have made such a choice in our favour. In fairness to my prior company, there must have been several cases (perhaps unknown to us) where they continued to retain the relationship when the CIO moved into a new setting. In conclusion, a company has to be blessed to win the faith and trust of customers like Aref and Mittu.

So what are the behaviours that build trust? We would say openness, transparency, proactive communication of bad news, honouring commitments, going the extra mile and always looking for ways to add additional value beyond the contract. It is important to understand the customer's business and the expectations of the customer's customer.

In your delivery of customer projects you will always strive for delivery excellence. But nothing in the world is perfect. Some things can and will go wrong. How you handle this situation can strengthen or destroy trust (remember the positive example in the B2C section).

Ashok recollects one such situation from his early MindTree days, which could have been a catastrophe but actually resulted in a series of victories:

Our US team had done an excellent job in winning a complex project to revamp Avis.com. The project was of critical importance to Avis. They were number two in world car rentals, but they lagged behind on Internet bookings while the market was rapidly shifting on to the Internet. The US team, comprising Joe King, Scott Staples, Anjan Lahiri and Erik Mann (all ex-Cambridge), had contributed to this win against giant incumbents and the latter two led the delivery. Though the project came in as IT, it was essentially a marketing project as Avis's future depended on it. Midway through the project, we heard rumblings of discontent on the progress and architecture of the solution. A new CIO, Raj Rawal, had joined Avis and rumour had it that MindTree was to be replaced as a partner. Subroto, who was based in the US then, called on Raj Rawal and took complete ownership of the responsibility for the dissonance in the mind of our customer's customer. He also said that we would work out a plan for restoring confidence and that I would personally present it. Subroto asked me to reach the US in a week, while detailed homework was done. We already knew that we had an A-team on the project with our best architect, Amit Agrawal, and our best business analyst, Chip Bearden. We asked our CTO, Kamran Ozair, to also get into troubleshooting mode when problems surfaced down the line. When I reached the US, we already had an entire plan ready to address their concerns. Specifically one of these was a concern on scalability, and we could demonstrate with confidence that the architecture would deliver on this front. We also set up a governance structure which included marketing. Raj decided to give us another chance and the rest was history for both Avis and MindTree. The solution helped Avis to rapidly grow its online business.

The successful completion of the project helped MindTree enter into several other Cendant group companies, and also Avis Europe, which brought us into contact with Mittu Sridhara, who later took both MindTree and Happiest Minds to multiple customers. Years later, Raj Rawal can still recall that what influenced him was Subroto taking complete responsibility without casting any aspersions on delayed inputs to our team, as well as the confidence we conveyed through our turnaround plan that the problems would not recur.

In many project executions, there will be situations where the team finds the cost and time of the project has been severely underestimated, or there are hurdles in the execution. In those times, line management under margin pressure may push to exit the project. Ashok's advice is:

Never, never walk away from a project. It will destroy trust and get you terrible negative publicity. During the MindTree days, we faced one such case with the Honda car company. The team began echoing the buyer on withdrawing, much to my concern. Fortunately, I found an ally in Raman, Honda's vice president. He knew me from my engineering days and sought a meeting with my team in Bangalore, which he wanted me to join. Our team entered the meeting with the intent of aborting the project. After my introductory remarks, Raman completely floored the team. He said, 'I want you to know that I am determined to see this project through with your team as I like your commitment and quality of work.' The mood in the room changed instantly. The BU head who had privately taken a strong stand to withdraw, led the way and said, 'Okay, let's see what the hurdles coming in the way are.' I excused myself from the meeting. Two hours later, Raman and the BU head walked in smiling to confirm that all details had been worked out to complete the project. What could have been the bitter end of a relationship led to happy project completion and multiple large orders for MindTree thereafter.

I should also recount the one and only case where I was involved in a failed relationship. The customer was a large media house in Delhi. Our team had grossly underestimated the project size. To make matters worse, our team felt that the customer had vastly enhanced the project requirements but were unwilling to pay for the changes. I decided to go to Delhi personally to save the relationship, with the mindset that we would absorb much of the costs of the overrun. The operating and senior management of the customer were present. I was surprised by the hostility of the operating leaders. They accused our team of dishonesty in demanding additional payment for changes which they felt were within the scope of the contract. Our team was adamant that this was not the case and also expressed distrust in the customer's team. Seeing this high level of mutual suspicion, I told the senior management of the media house that they could keep all the deliverables to date without paying us and complete the project with some other partner. To the best of our knowledge, the quotation they received was three times higher than ours (while we were requesting a 50 per cent increase) and they never went ahead with the project. Still, I hold us responsible. The project specification should have been vetted in such a way that there was no possibility of anyone forming a different interpretation of the deliverables. The lesson: sometimes teams are so excited about winning business that they rush in without due diligence on the documentation—only to discover later that the devil is in the details.

One of the concerns when you start a B2B business is how you will convince customers to give you business when the company has not yet established a track record. Fortunately, Ashok has found that for the first two years, the customer is willing to include the experience of team members while evaluating a new partner. After that, there is a sudden shift and they want to know what you have delivered as a company. That's why at Happiest Minds we focused on getting new accounts in the beginning, and within two years had a customer base of over 100 and could demonstrate the execution of several hundred challenging use cases.

The following is a list of approaches we have found to be helpful in making an entry with B2B customers to build confidence in your capabilities:

- Offer to do a proof of concept prior to being awarded the full project.
- Present a convincing point of view (PoV) on issues or technology choices where the customer is having a hard time making a choice.
- Approach the innovation team and suggest some breakthrough concepts. The innovation folks usually have the freedom to look at new partners, whereas conventional IT teams have existing gatekeepers in the

form of vendor development and will frequently say 'we have enough partners'.

- Offer to co-create a solution with a customer. In such cases you may offer a cost-plus price, but you retain the intellectual property (IP) and give the customer a royalty on subsequent sales to other customers.

One model for winning business which we would strongly suggest you to avoid is the build-operate-transfer (BOT) model. In B2B businesses your objective is to develop annuity revenues through long-lasting relationships with customers. It's a pity to do the hard work of building a team and hand the team and work over when it is poised for further growth. During Ashok's stint in Wipro, Dun & Bradstreet (D&B) came to India with a BOT proposal. The shortlisted partners were Wipro, as the preferred partner, and Satyam. Ashok had hoped to persuade D&B for a different approach than BOT. D&B realized this, and the deal went to Satyam who gladly accepted the offer. A few years later, D&B exercised the BOT option and transferred all the business to a new entity. This was how Cognizant, one of the most formidable players in the industry, was born. Another example: while MindTree was negotiating the acquisition of Aztecsoft, their largest customer exercised the BOT clause in their contract. The result—a big decline in revenue, profit and share price, enabling a good buyout price for MindTree.

There is also a noticeable trend of consumerization in IT. This means that the technologies which were initially used only for B2C sales are now finding application in B2B environments. Accordingly, B2B CIOs and chief marketing officers (CMOs) are increasingly using analytics and other data services to:

- Microsegment the target market
- Create a picture of the ideal customer profile

- Target likely buyers
- Lead nurturing by customized content
- Prioritize sales leads and predict the likelihood of closing deals
- Identify account-specific influences
- Have better account-based marketing to grow existing accounts

Finally, a very important influencer in B2B marketing is thought leadership as recognized by industry analysts, and intellectual property, particularly if this can give the customer a competitive differentiation.

The Future of Marketing

Up till now, the technologies in use have aimed to collate more information about the customer in real time. Much of this, by way of digitization, has been intrusive at the cost of customer experience. Our colleague, Gopala Krishna Seruku (G.K.), the customer experience professional at Happiest Minds, has published a couple of articles on LinkedIn responding to this dilemma, and has noticed the following common attributes of customer-focused organizations:

- Committing to customer success
- Engaging with customers from the get-go
- Committing to customers from the top-down
- Engendering a customer-centric culture
- Recognizing the customer across all lines of business
- Designing processes and policies from the customer's point of view
- Measuring what matters to customers
- Encouraging customer innovation

G.K. found that highly focused customer-experience firms had fine-tuned their processes, starting with customer on-boarding, employee empowerment and sales returns, towards improving customer experience. An amazing example for creating a customer-oriented culture is a company where employees do not have sales targets, but are incentivized for enhancing the customer experience.

We leave predictions on the future of marketing to the gurus. However, as customers ourselves, we feel that the next major change in marketing will be to use the same digital technologies to vastly improve customer experience, to demonstrate to the customer that 'we care'. Those who do this well will be the winners.

KEY TAKEAWAYS

✓ Building a brand begins with the company name, which should be interesting and memorable. The brand has both market and supply elements which must be consistent and complementary. All brand extensions should be consistent with the company's brand promise.

✓ The best publicity is free publicity. Third-party statements such as media articles and social media comments have higher credibility than your own statements or paid advertisements. Customer testimonials are the most powerful publicity. To get a vast amount of free coverage, 'be interesting, do interesting'.

✓ In a content-driven world, the team must project its capability through articles in reputed journals, blogs etc.

✓ In a digital world, permission marketing has given way to intrusive marketing, which includes proximity marketing, predictive marketing, context-aware marketing etc. This new power of consumer access in an interconnected world has to be wielded with care.

✓ Small marketing budgets can spur creativity within the marketing team, leading to focused efforts rather than spray-and-pray approaches.

✓ Building trust is important in both B2B and B2C marketing. When things go wrong, handle these exceptions well as they can contribute to building trust.

✓ In a digital world, platformization of your offerings is also important in both B2B and B2C worlds. In B2C, it helps in generating annuity revenue through 'software as a service' delivery. In B2B, highly scalable platforms help in rapid business expansion.

✓ Leverage the go-to-market programmes of large partners.

✓ The name of the game in B2C marketing is to be the lead adopters of the latest technologies, which give more and more real-time information on their customers. These technologies include predictive analytics, algorithms, big data analysis, Internet of things, artificial intelligence and machine-to-machine learning.

✓ Omnichannel approaches are increasingly popular in reaching B2C customers.

✓ Excessive choice in pricing, schemes and product variety can confuse a customer and lead to delays in decision-making. Keep it simple.

✓ Most people think of marketing as either B2B or B2C, but there is a third category of B2B2C. In this category, the service provider uses the intermediate 'B' as a demand aggregator and leverages its customer affinity partnerships. It is also like a B2C sale as the service provider has to fulfil the needs and expectations of each individual consumer and also requires a scalable engagement platform. B2B2C can evolve into B2C and the two models need not be mutually exclusive.

✓ In B2B sales, your first few customers are truly special and deserve a lifetime of gratitude. They help to validate that you have an offering of interest to customers.

✓ B2B marketing can contribute directly to sales through a website which draws in business inquiries, leading positions on search engine lists etc.

✓ B2B business is brought through trust, past relationships, offering to demonstrate capability through proofs of concept, and asking for work on the frontiers of innovation.

✓ The behaviours which build trust are openness, transparency, proactive communication of bad news, honouring commitments, going the extra mile and adding value beyond the contract. As noted earlier, how you handle matters when things go wrong is of great importance.

✓ Never walk away from a project because you have underestimated the size and have huge overruns. On the flip side, if the customer has significantly enhanced specifications, you have a right to expect your dues and there is no need to work for free. If project specifications are ambiguous or open to interpretation, it is your responsibility to do the due diligence since you are the expert who should have defined things unambiguously.

✓ For the first two years in a B2B business, the customer will be willing to evaluate you based on the past track record and experience of your team. After that, they will assess you based on what your company has delivered. Hence the need to quickly develop a profile of multiple challenging and innovative use cases.

- ✓ Approaches useful for account entry in a B2B business include proof of concept, convincing points of view (PoV), thought leadership, partnering through innovation, co-creation with customers and IP-based sales.
- ✓ An approach to be avoided for winning business is build-operate-transfer (BOT).
- ✓ Consumerization of IT is leading to similar technologies being used in the corporate environment and data sciences becoming prevalent in B2B solutions.
- ✓ In the future, marketers will compensate for their intrusiveness by using digital technologies to vastly improve the customers' experience and demonstrate that 'we care'.

8.

Wealth Creation and Sharing

'It is not how much money you make, but how much money you keep, how hard it works for you and how many generations you keep it for'

—Robert Kiyosaki

Before you think of how you will share or divide the wealth pie, your single-minded goal should be how to increase the size of the pie. All the chapters in this book give you takeaways for increasing the size of the pie, which begins with having VCs who will help you add value and the right founding team to your venture. Of course, you may decide not to go for external funding, but our belief is that good VCs can help you increase the total value of your company. Regarding the founding team, the best example we can give is of the large founding team at Infosys. Narayana Murthy could have retained a larger share of equity for himself by having fewer founders. By opting to have an A-team of seven founders, he was able to build a company of $20 billion-plus valuation—much better even for his own wealth creation than, say, having three founders but creating only a $5 billion market-cap company. Admittedly, the arithmetic is not that simple as a large initial team does not always lead to a larger valuation and a large founding team may not always work out. The purpose here is just to reinforce the point that while selecting VCs and the founding team, first think of how to create a large pie and only next think of how best to divide it.

If the company performs well, the VCs will definitely get a good return on the capital invested. Likewise, the founders should also generate significant wealth. But unfortunately, there are cases where the company has done well, the VCs have made money and yet the founders have made very little for themselves. A recurring reason is that in order to raise funds, founders end up parting with too much equity. As discussed previously, we do recommend that founders plan to close the pre-IPO funding round with control of at least 40 per cent of the equity. It is important to carefully scrutinize shareholder agreements and related documents to guard against clauses which can give founders a haircut.

Employee Stock Option Plan (ESOP)

We now come to the largest category of stakeholders whose wealth creation as the entrepreneur, you need to plan for: the employees who help to build your organization. The most common (and best) way of rewarding employees is through a well-drafted stock option plan, commonly referred to as an ESOP, which reflects your philosophy for wealth sharing. In the sections which follow, we will discuss issues like what percentage of the stock should be reserved for the ESOP scheme, how to protect the company's interests even while having a generous ESOP allocation, how to ensure that gains for employees are not frittered away by paying income tax, which could have been saved with a well-drafted ESOP scheme, and ensuring timely actions by employees for exercising their options or making suitable declarations to the appropriate authorities. It should be remembered that the rules governing taxation on ESOPs vary from country to country and also change from time to time. Accordingly, you will be well advised to engage with reputed lawyers in each country in which you have significant team sizes. Employees are generally naive about what is the best action for them to take, as the ESOP documents themselves and the rules governing them are complex. In some countries, especially litigious ones like the US, there is concern about giving advice to employees on areas like when to exercise the stock option and so on, in case it later turns out to be non-beneficial to the employee. It is our view that it is best to lay down the facts simply and also include a set of frequently asked questions (FAQs). The appropriate approach then becomes self-evident, but the company should not be directive and instead, should qualify the responses by encouraging employees to seek legal advice on what is best for their own interests.

Percentage of Stocks for ESOP Scheme and Coverage

The most common percentage of the ESOP pool to the undiluted stock is 20 per cent, which comes down to 16.67 per cent of the total stock after the ESOP stock is added. In Silicon Valley, this is almost a universal practice and is recommended by VCs. In some cases ESOP stock even goes up to 25 per cent (undiluted) and 20 per cent net. In India we have found many organizations parting with much less, but we do believe that an adequate stock pool should be created for employees.

Regarding coverage, most product start-ups with small teams tend to cover the entire team, while companies with large team sizes like services companies or e-commerce companies are more selective and may restrict ESOPs to only the leadership team. Since the pool size is finite, the latter approach, compared to universal coverage, allows for higher stocks and higher wealth creation for only a few.

Ashok's philosophy on stock options has been that all those who contribute to building the company in its early years, say the first three to four years, should be covered under the ESOP scheme. This creates a sense of ownership and also promotes alignment with the company's goals. Initially at MindTree, everyone was covered by ESOPs from the entry level onwards, and this continued till there were as many as 500 persons on the payroll. At Happiest Minds, the investment base was much larger, and the ESOP pool was enhanced from 16.67 per cent to 20 per cent. This enabled universal coverage to continue till the company reached a team size of about 1800 persons at the end of the fourth full financial year. However, since Ashok wanted the rewards to go to those who had helped to take the company to IPO, a clause was added requiring employees leaving the company pre-IPO or after seven years, whichever was earlier, to return even the vested stocks at the last issue price. Though not part of the plan, exceptions were made for those who were asked to leave and they were allowed to retain some or all of their vested stocks, so that they had some share in the value they had helped create while in the company. Furthermore, for the first four years the issue price was increased very marginally. This served a dual purpose: later entrants got a per share gain opportunity which was almost as much as the early joinees, and those who left didn't walk away with shares that would have continued to appreciate long after their contributions had ceased.

Planning the ESOP Allocations and Replenishing the ESOP Pool

The ESOP programme is a costly one and what, when and how much of the stock options to distribute needs to be planned well. In the chapter on funding your venture, we advised you to assess the total funding you are likely to need and work backwards on how to stagger this amount between series A, B and other follow-up rounds. Likewise, with ESOPs, you must determine the total pool you are likely to need and work out a grid based on the grade of the employee, which is based on the employee's position in the company. The grade-wise quantum is not fixed forever. After every six months or one year the quantum of shares per person in each grade can be reduced, as the earliest joinees have taken the highest risk of joining a start-up and deserve a higher stock award. Such advance planning is needed to ensure you still have an adequate ESOP pool available to attract talent several years after start-up.

The ESOP pool can be augmented whenever there is a new fundraising round, but it is preferable to grant the maximum quantum possible at the start-up stage when the issue price is at its lowest. When an employee leaves the company, the unvested stocks get cancelled and the pool gets replenished. If you opt for the feature mentioned above whereby resigning employees have to sell back their vested stock to the company, the ESOP pool gets further replenished through attrition. You could make the buy-back clause more attractive to employees by linking it to the fair market value instead of the last issue price. The buy-back does involve a cash outflow for the company. Accordingly, you can make it compulsory for the departing employee to surrender the stock, but optional for the company to exercise its right to buy-back.

If there is no buy-back provision, once an employee decides to leave, he or she should be required to exercise all unexercised options within a predefined period, typically sixty days.

An award to the employee should always be stated in terms of the number of shares and not in terms of percentage of the company. This is to avoid ambiguity; also, stating the award in percentage terms may lead to unintended or disproportionate gains as fresh shares have to be issued to employees whenever there is a new issue.

Usually, the share base of the company needs to be increased so that every employee gets a reasonable number of shares. One way in which this is done is after the VCs invest in the company, the premium is used for increasing the share capital base through the issue of bonus shares. The shares can also be split, for example, by reducing the par value from Rs 10 to Rs 2. Some organizations reduce value even below the par value of Re 1, but this is not recommended because stocks with a par value of below Rs 2 cannot be easily listed on the stock exchange outside India (say, in the US, where the typical par value is 5 cents, which is equivalent roughly to Rs 3 in 2016). Even in India, the minimum par value needed to list on a stock exchange is Re 1.

Monetizing ESOP Gains for Employees

A number of employees are sceptical about the value and attractiveness of ESOPs because they see these as paper investments with limited likelihood for monetizing and that too, in the distant future. Also, given the failure rate of start-ups, there is reasonable probability that employees will not gain much or really anything from ESOPs, so often employees tend to be wary of such schemes. They will not be willing to consider the expected value as part of their compensation, but will like to see it as the icing on the cake when things go well.

Notwithstanding the above, we firmly believe that ESOPs are the best way for the team to participate in a company's success—and you start a company with a view to make it a success. ESOPs must be granted when people join, as deferring the issue of stock creates other problems. For example, over time, the ESOP grant price will need to increase in line with the fair market value (FMV), reducing the gains for employees. If you choose to issue the options at lower than FMV, the gap will be treated as a cost to the company and the expense a debit to your P & L.

In order to create earlier liquidity for employees, some companies include the following features in their ESOP programmes:

- A provision is included to encash the vested stock whenever there is a liquidity event such as the company being acquired. Such a provision can also be accompanied by accelerated vesting of options.
- Employees can be given the right to encash a part of their holdings during subsequent rounds of financing.
- Companies which are doing well can create a private market of sorts through an Employee Benefit Trust Fund. (Flipkart is a recent example.) This gives employees the opportunity to convert a part of their vested stock into cash.

However, all the above-mentioned methods of monetizing options will attract an income tax levy of 20 per cent subject to the stock being held for at least two years after exercise. Indexation benefits are also available which may reduce the tax burden. Our preferred methodology for monetizing gains is after IPO, when stocks held for a minimum of one year can be sold on the market without any capital gains tax.

Taxation and Related Issues for ESOP Schemes

Taxation issues can be complex and the approach to taxation varies from country to country. One major feature of Indian rules on ESOP taxation is that employees are taxed at the time of exercise by the employees. The difference between the value of the stock at the time of exercise and the option grant price is required to be withheld as tax on perquisites in the hands of the employee. In a start-up, till IPO the shares are not liquid at the time of exercise. This means that the employee has to pay tax on an unrealized gain. If there is a down-round after exercising, the employee loses both ways as he or she has already paid tax based on a higher price.

In the US and the UK and probably in most other countries, stock options are typically taxed at the time of sale. However, there are important elections/declarations employees have to make while acquiring stock either at the time of grant or through early exercise (as applicable), which can have an impact on taxability. The US, in particular, has complex rules and you need a specific stock option plan called the Incentive Stock Option (ISO) plan to get the benefit of deferring bulk of the tax till sale.

Below, Ashok describes the complications which occurred when ESOP schemes were started at MindTree and how the learning helped him get it right in India the second time round when Happiest Minds was established:

When we created the US-based ESOP scheme at MindTree, we wanted to retain the flexibility of issuing stocks at less than fair market value (FMV). What we didn't realize was that this well-meaning intent made our stock option plan a Non-Qualified Plan under US law. In the US, certain tax exemptions for US residents are applicable only for those under a Qualified Plan. Not surprisingly, the plan we had adopted created a lot of heartburn with our US team, but by then it was too late to rectify the situation.

In the US, there is also an issue of restricted versus unrestricted stock or vested versus unvested stock. While tax liability has to be paid at the time of vesting in the case of restricted stock, this liability can be deferred till sale if the stock is issued under an ISO plan. Our condition of buying back the stock at the last issue price led to our stock being classified as restricted. For it to be unrestricted, we should have either allowed employees to retain the stock on cessation of employment or provided buy-back at FMV as an option.

Buy-back at the last issue price was an important clause for us at Happiest Minds in view of the giant-sized ESOP pool. Since it also worked in favour of the employee for tax considerations, we retained this clause. The US also requires compliance with Section 409A of the Internal Revenue Code and specifies qualifying conditions for deferring income and taxation. You will be well advised to understand all these aspects and engage a lawyer who helps you create a scheme optimized in accordance with your goals and employee taxability.

While we got all the parameters of the scheme right in drawing up the Happiest Minds ESOP scheme, we were anxious not to be directive in our recommendations and this contributed to some members of our US team not electing to make a required election and declaration within the specified period. In the US when employees are offered unvested restricted stock, they are permitted, under Section 83(b) of the Internal Revenue Code of the US, to elect to recognize income at the time of acquisition of the stock (as opposed to recognizing income at the time of vesting) for the same and make a self-declaration to the IRS within thirty days of grant of the restricted stock to lock in the price. Subsequently, the bulk of the tax is deferred to sale. If this is not done, it apparently leads to the levy of taxes when the stock vests and the market price is higher than the price paid for acquisition. Ironically, it was our senior-most persons (other than the CEO & MD) who also missed out on the election and self-declaration. At the time of writing this book, we are still unsure of how this innocent omission will play out in terms of taxability for the concerned persons.

The situation in the UK is simpler and the Indian ESOP applies there. However, here also employees need to be made aware of declarations required by Her Majesty's Revenue and Customs (HMRC) and its impact on taxability.

One action we took which helped us globally was that initially, we issued all ESOPs at the par value of Rs 2 (equivalent to about 4 cents in the US at that time). Within the first six months, we had issued almost 65 per cent of our large ESOP pool. In India, we took further action to actively encourage and advise employees to immediately exercise their options and thereby become stockholders. On exercise of options, employees did have a cash outflow, but since the price was low, it was very affordable. For those shareholders who stay on till the IPO, if they sell the stocks on the stock market, there will hopefully be only a securities transaction tax and no capital gains tax. We do believe this scheme developed by our legal counsel, Rajiv Khaitan of Khaitan & Co and Gopalan, is a truly optimal scheme for both our company and employees under current Indian taxation laws.

Gopalan adds an important reminder for the management: when employees exercise their options, they attain the status of shareholders of your company and you should treat them at par with any shareholder.

In conclusion, your company's ESOP scheme should be the most important vehicle for wealth generation for your team. It is a 'high cost to company scheme' and needs careful deliberation to create a scheme which safeguards company interests but is also optimized for employees in all jurisdictions in which the company operates, particularly from the point of view of their personal cash flow and taxability.

KEY TAKEAWAYS

- ✓ The first priority is to increase the size of the pie before you think of how to divide and share it.
- ✓ VCs will always make money if the company performs well. There are cases where even though the company has done well, the founders have made little. We recommend that founders close the pre-IPO round with a minimum of 40 per cent of the equity. Also, ensure the non-inclusion of clauses in the shareholders' agreement which can give founders a haircut.
- ✓ The Employee Stock Option Plan is your main vehicle for employee wealth creation. In Silicon Valley, most companies reserve 16.67 to 20 per cent of the diluted stock. In India, many companies tend to reserve a lower percentage.
- ✓ Product companies tend to cover all early-stage employees with options, while services and e-commerce companies tend to be more selective and give stock awards to only senior management or the leadership team.
- ✓ We recommend a stock option pool of at least 16.67 per cent and also coverage of all employees who join

in the first two to four years of start-up. This approach ensures alignment of goals between employees and the company while giving everybody a sense of ownership.

✓ We also recommend the inclusion of a clause that persons who leave prior to a predetermined period be required to return the vested stock to the company, while the company itself is not obligated to buy-back. The period for compulsory return of stock can be five to seven years after joining or the IPO, whichever is earlier. The buy-back price can be the last issue price or the fair market value, of which the latter is obviously more generous to employees.

✓ ESOP distribution needs to be well planned based on a grade-wise grid, where an employee's allotment in a particular grade is highest at inception and reduces gradually.

✓ Some people are sceptical about ESOP plans for wealth creation since there are limited avenues for monetization, high probability of failure and the IPO seems too far away. In order to improve liquidity for employees, they can be given the opportunity to encash their stocks whenever there is a liquidity event or by creation of an employee benefit trust.

✓ Our preferred methodology for monetizing gains is after the IPO, where stock held for a minimum of one year can be sold on the market without any capital gains tax.

✓ In India, unlike in the US or the UK, employees are taxed at the time of option exercise, which means the employee gets taxed on an unrealized gain. To counter this inequity, the best approach is to issue a large proportion of the equity pool right at the beginning at a par price of, say, Rs 2 and to encourage employees to exercise their options immediately and convert them into stocks. Though this involves an early cash outflow for the employee, the amount per share is small and this will optimize the income tax impact on the employee in future years.

✓ Many countries have their own rules for stock options. The US in particular requires a separate stock option plan conforming to their rules. Issues which you need to understand from your lawyers include the Qualified versus Non-Qualified Plan, Restricted versus Non-restricted stock and Section 409A compliance and elections under Section 83(b). All these can have an impact on the taxability of employees.

✓ Though both the US and the UK tax options typically at the time of sale, both require elections and/or declarations by employees within a finite period to the respective revenue/taxation authorities. It is important to educate and guide employees regarding such requirements without being overly directive to avoid litigation if things do not work out as per expectations.

✓ When employees exercise their stock options, they attain the status of shareholders and should be treated on par with other shareholders.

✓ Your ESOP scheme is your most important vehicle for wealth generation for your employees. It is also a high-cost scheme and needs careful deliberation so that you create a scheme which safeguards the company's interests, but is also optimized from the cash flow and taxability angles of employees in various jurisdictions.

9.

Strategic Sale of Your Company

'Some people believe holding on and hanging in there are signs of great strength. However, there are times when it takes much more strength to know when to let go and then do it'

—Ann Landers, American advice columnist

'And the day came when the risk to remain tight in a bud was more painful than the risk it took to blossom'

—Anais Nin

'In business, you don't get what you deserve, you get what you negotiate'

—Anonymous

Parting with a Prized Possession

When a group of people start a venture, they have dreams about its future—very much like parents having ambitions for their children. In fact, the venture is their baby and, like parents, they will make enormous sacrifices to nurture it. Very few consciously think about an exit plan for themselves or their investors. Whenever I address a gathering of entrepreneurs at TiE or NASSCOM or other fora, I ask how many would like to eventually take their companies public. About 20 per cent put up their hands. The sad truth is that many will never realize this dream. Taking a company public requires scale, predictability of revenues and profits, and the ability to withstand the unforgiving, relentless glare of public scrutiny. The balance 80 per cent have seldom given thought to an exit strategy, and this is treated as something they will address, if and when required. If you have taken external investments and already done multiple rounds, you will have to give your investors an exit as this route for raising funds for growth will dry up. If you have bootstrapped your company, you will also want to monetize your investments. In the US and, increasingly, in India too, absence of profits need not be a deterrent, and you can hold on to your company if you demonstrate high growth and scalability. Very large number of the unicorns fit into this category.

There is also a need to pay yourselves a decent salary as most start-up entrepreneurs pay themselves a fraction of what they could earn in a large organization. This leads to years of skimping to make ends meet. There, however, are exceptions of companies which took no external funds and went on to build large, profitable enterprises which can also afford a generous compensation to the founders. Such companies can remain private. Examples include Serum Institute, Patanjali, Cargill and Ferrero. However, these are the rare exceptions.

As you face reality, it will dawn on you that you have no option but a strategic sale. There will be happiness that you are placing your baby in stronger, powerful hands to help it grow. However, there will also be a strong sense of loss. Your company will no longer remain an independent entity. There will be a change in your role and probably those of several other senior team members too. In effect, it will be a highly emotive decision where you will experience many highs and lows. This is the time to remember Anais Nin's advice above, *'And the day came when the risk to remain tight in a bud was more painful than the risk it took to blossom.'*

Why and When You Should Plan a Strategic Sale

Business is about creating value for all stakeholders. This requires scale, cash flow and profitability. You may feel you are approaching a state where you can't go to the market for another round of funding and you have examined all possible strategic options including pivoting. You may also know deep inside by now that there are other organizations that can add much greater value to, and realize the potential of, your product or service. The time to act is sooner than later. The worst time to seek a buyer is when you are almost out of cash, and in danger of defaulting on payments and salaries. If you hold on till too late, the sale will be a distress effort to avoid bankruptcy. Though you don't want to be a quitter, there will be a time when the risk of holding on will far exceed the potential benefit. You may also figure out that your entity is ripe to take off, and putting it up for acquisition will provide wings to your and your team's aspirations. This is particularly true if you are in a hot space. At the time of writing, such spaces include edutech, e-health and predictive analytics to name only a few.

Never do your strategic sale with your back to the wall. The right buyer will not be available at the drop of a hat. The acquisition process will require due diligence. Accordingly, you need to allow eight to twelve months for the search. There are companies that specialize in looking out for start-ups in distress to get a bargain basement price. Don't allow yourself to become such a target.

There is one positive situation where the strategic sale can be a big win for you and your team. You have an even better idea for a new business. The proceeds from your strategic sale can be mostly poured into your new venture to give you a higher percentage of ownership.

Either way, you must have an end goal and start working towards creating a new future.

Should You Start a Company with a View to Selling the Same?

Many gurus will say that you should never start a company with a view to selling it. I would differ, but only if you are focused on creating value. When you are planning from the inception to sell your company, you are not only creating value but also making yourself valuable to a possible range of buyers.

However, my advice would be to always give yourself flexibility. Even if you have built your company with a view to sell, keep your options open to go public or even to become an acquirer, if possible. As long as you are creating value while you run your company, different strategic options will appear.

Which type of companies and what type of value creation lend themselves for a strategic sale? I will illustrate two variations with examples:

The first is when you are a superb technology and design team, and are building an excellent product or platform. You also know that to realize the business potential of the platform is not your forte, and that it needs an entity with established market channels and customers. In the section on serial entrepreneurship in the appendix to this book, I have given the example of Prem Jain, a serial entrepreneur in Silicon Valley. I am reproducing my own words from that section:

> . . . Prem Jain, a brilliant engineer, realized that his skill lay in creating new products but it was not his forte to run companies and scale them to their potential. He sold his first company to Cisco. Later, along with few other colleagues, he stepped out of Cisco to start Nuova Systems. In the pressure-cooker atmosphere of a start-up, they were able to develop a next generation server and a switching product, found an eager acquirer in Cisco again, where the product soon became a billion dollar-plus category. This approach was so successful that Prem and his friends repeated it by starting Insieme Networks and again finding a ready suitor at Cisco.

Though Prem and his partners sold their companies to Cisco, they obviously also had a choice of other networking and intelligent infrastructure product companies. Developing the product in a start-up gave them speed in terms of readiness and reduction in time to market. And obviously, this should have been great for the designing team in terms of wealth creation!

The other example is the more common or frequent one. The large companies, particularly high-tech ones, are always on the lookout for acquisitions. They know that some of the most cutting-edge technology developments are done within start-ups. Companies like Microsoft and Cisco would have done well above 100 or even 200 acquisitions combined during the years. They all face relentless pressure for continued growth, and acquisitions that fit into the white spaces of their portfolios are great additions. The acquisition could also be a bolt on to the parent. The founders of WhatsApp may not have created the company for resale, but they must have gone laughing all the way to the bank when they found Facebook as a buyer for a cool sum around $20 billion.

With new technologies being developed into solutions in India, many MNCs also regularly scan the Indian scene for acquisition targets. Furthermore, larger Indian players, particularly the unicorns, are looking at companies aggressively to increase their own growth and market cap. The most recent example is Byju's, already valued at $10 billion at the time of writing, having acquired the new coding edutech start-up WhiteHat Jr. One additional advantage for the sellers in the WhiteHat deal is that it seems Byju's is going to keep WhiteHat as a separate entity. The founding CEO will be allowed to keep managing the same, but now under the Byju's umbrella. The large customer base of Byju's becomes an immediate target for WhiteHat to cross-sell its services.

The one major positive in selling your company to a cash-rich player is that it's a much faster path to wealth creation than an IPO. However, once you have sold your company, you don't participate in future wealth creation unless you negotiate a part-cash and part-equity deal.

How Do You Find a Buyer and to Whom Do You Sell?

We live in a thriving ecosystem for entrepreneurs. If you have created value, word will get around through this ecosystem. Odds are you will have already received multiple feelers through investment bankers to check if you are interested in being acquired. More often it is phrased as, 'Are you open to a merger?' This is to let you feel you are not going to be swallowed whole. If you have taken external funds, your VCs or private equity partners will be your allies in finding a buyer for you and facilitating their own exit. You can also consider giving a mandate to an investment banker for finding you a buyer.

However, it's far better to have someone beat a path to your door than to go around shopping for a buyer. It makes your enterprise a more attractive target. At times, you could select a few potential acquirers yourself amongst entities you know in your industry and approach them directly.

Many years ago, while leading MindTree, I was pleasantly surprised to receive a call from K.B. Chandrasekhar (KBC), chairman and promoter of Aztecsoft. KBC had been a part of my team in Wipro and was looking to divest Aztecsoft. I am sure he spoke to other potential buyers also, but after just two rounds of discussions we were able to close the deal with no intermediaries involved. From KBC's angle, this was an example of leveraging his own contacts, built during his years of being a serial entrepreneur. When you are looking to sell your venture, you should also build your relationships with potential buyers. If I may make a small detour from this story to mention an unplanned benefit to me from MindTree acquiring Aztecsoft. Three of its senior team members (Joseph Anantharaju, Aurobinda Nanda and Sridhar Mantha) are part of my top management at Happiest Minds. Furthermore, many of the outstanding technology professionals in our product engineering business also joined Happiest Minds with Nanda.

Coming back to your considerations for selling your venture. Valuation and price are obvious factors. However, these should not be the only factor. I believe a key consideration should be which buyer will provide the best home for your team. Do you see a culture match which will lead to successful integration? Will your team be welcomed as equals to their peers in the new system and given a fair chance of being selected for certain key roles where the integration of the two organizations will create duplications requiring rationalization? I have no idea what other offers KBC had on the table when he brought Aztecsoft to MindTree. What I am sure of is that he chose us because he saw that we would be the best home for his team. Though I have never sold any enterprise, I did use this principle when I was selling my MindTree shares at exit. Lip-Bu Tan, of Walden, and I were the two largest shareholders by far. Lip-Bu had told me that he would sell his shares to whomever I chose. We had strong expressions of interest from two large entities. However, I suggested to Siddhartha (of Café Coffee Day and an investor in MindTree) that he buy our shares, and he became their white knight until shortly before his tragic death. This allowed my erstwhile colleagues to retain and manage their own homes for almost ten more years.

Valuation of Your Enterprise

This is the time when the standard rules of valuation like projected cash flow and profits have to be thrown out of the window. What matters is what strategic benefits your organization creates for the buyer and what the buyer can achieve through your organization in terms of the above parameters of profitability, etc. Obviously, the organization best positioned to make these assessments is the buyer, but you must also be able to make a fair estimate to confidently demand and negotiate the best price. The best example of this is Walmart's acquisition of Flipkart. The latter was faced with a global gorilla. Sooner or later, like its other domestic peers, its growth would have stalled. At the time of the acquisition, Flipkart was still holding out well. Walmart, the largest retailer in the world, was seeing the inexorable growth of Amazon in the US market, grabbing market share from retailers in one segment after another. Walmart desperately needed an e-commerce platform in a large consumer market. What country better than India and which company better than Flipkart. Once these imperatives are understood, the price of $22 billion, which was settled for the Flipkart negotiation, doesn't seem too high; in fact, maybe not high enough! At the time of writing, there are, to my mind, indications that Flipkart is preparing for a US listing which, I expect, will show that the procurement price was a steal.

The conventional methods of valuation do come into play when you are selling a services company. The usual parameters of revenue, EBITDA and the growth rate of both will be important. For this you will give future projections. Odds are that these will be more optimistic than your past growth rates justify. The buyer will discount these and do a valuation exercise. This can be through one or all of several methods, such as discounted cash flow, comparable company valuations and precedent transactions. The buyer will then make you an offer, and this is where the art of negotiation will begin. You have to put yourself in the mind of the buyer. If you assess that they see high strategic value in acquiring your company, you can make your case for a much higher valuation than their offer.

Another aspect of valuation is that your buyer may want to pay you part cash and part earnout based on projections you have provided. Earnout criteria become difficult to measure once an organization is integrated with the parent. My experience has been that earnout structures often reduce strategic flexibility (e.g. reorganization) for the buyer and concerns for the seller who may feel that effective control on results is now dependent on the larger system and not just on the selling team's performance. Also, it's important to keep the deal simple. Don't try to overoptimize on tax savings etc., as this can lead to years of complications. Finally, good corporate governance will always fetch you a premium. Don't cut corners and choose expedient approaches while you grow your company. Such acts will hit back and bite you later. Do remember that the sale process is a distractor for top management and will impact the time you have for building your business. Accordingly, it's best to keep the process as swift as logically possible.

A good valuation will generate wealth for you and your co-founders. This is also a good time to share some of this wealth with key senior persons who have helped you build this wealth, including those who may not be covered with stock options. I have not noticed this generosity of spirit in many divestments. In this regard, I would like to mention Ajay Agrawal, CEO of Cupola, who widely shared the proceeds from the sale with a significant number of his team.

Valuation is often described as part science and part art. If you are selling intellectual property or a technology platform or even a new future for the buyer, I believe it's all art. You will have to build your story around your differentiators, particularly with respect to your comparator companies, the capabilities and IP you have built, and the scalability and future-proofing of your platform. Finally, it will greatly help in negotiations if you have more than one suitor.

Planning Your Future Career

I have done six acquisitions in my career. In all but one, the CEO moved on within a short period after the acquisition. Likewise, many of the senior team members cannot adjust to the new environment and also leave after some time or when earnouts are completed. The happy exception is our buyout of Cupola at Happiest Minds. The CEO, Ajay Agrawal, has adapted well to his new role as head of the Centre of Excellence for Analytics and AI. His co-founder, Saifee Huzefa, settled into a role which gave him a larger canvas. Almost all the other key persons in the Cupola team are still with us, more than three years after completing the acquisition. Apart from my own experience, I have witnessed the departure of the acquired company's

CEO in dozens of cases. However, Som Mittal, my erstwhile colleague from the Wipro days, was twice selected as the CEO of the acquiring company instead of the incumbent CEO at the acquirer.

The reason for CEO discontent is evident. The authority of a company CEO as compared to a business unit (BU) head is more complete. The major frustration for acquired company CEOs is due to centralized functions like finance, people, marketing, etc. Decisions for a BU have to take into account the existence of other BUs and their priorities. Accordingly, many decisions which a CEO made on his own now get raised for socialization with the new company CEO and a committee of peers. The CEO finds this frustrating, feels the organization is slow and bureaucratic. Also, the structure, processes and mode of decision making in the buying enterprise may not suit the CEO's entrepreneurial style of working. The reason Ajay has adapted is that he also is a techie at heart, and the new technological challenges of our Analytics CoE engaged him and rekindled his passion. While he was also a good CEO in Cupola, at Happiest Minds he got an excellent opportunity to revert to his original love and forte, without the headaches of keeping his company going in the tight financial constraints under which most start-ups operate.

The bottom line is that if you are a CEO of a company, you will find it difficult to adjust. You may also not have a place in the new set-up, and after a brief transition period, you would have to move on. In either event, you have to plan a career ahead. The best way to overcome the sense of loss on giving up the company you created is to plan for something new and exciting. This planning and searching should go on in parallel with your efforts to sell your company, and the efforts should be stepped up soon as the deal is secured. However, there is a chance that you can be like Ajay and enjoy a new challenge within the new set-up, in which case that itself can be a new beginning for you.

KEY TAKEAWAYS

✓ Strategic sale of a venture is the most common exit route for founders and also for investors. The reason is that most organizations cannot build adequate scale and predictability of growth/profitability to do an IPO.

✓ For founders, the sale of the venture is an emotive decision. There will be happiness and a strong sense of loss.

✓ The right buyer will be able to realize far greater value for the organization you built.

✓ Strategic sales take time to implement, and you should start your lookout eight to twelve months before the survival of your venture becomes a grave threat. Don't get yourself in the position where you have to make a distress sale.

✓ It is okay to start a company with the objective of selling the same, but only if you remain focused on creating value. Also, even for such a venture, keep your options open for becoming the consolidator (rather than getting acquired) or take the organization on to an IPO.

✓ The best prospects for getting high value from a strategic sale are when you have created intellectual property, be it a product or platform. Valuation will also be high if your company fulfils a strategic objective for the buyer. Good corporate governance will always get you a valuation premium.

✓ There are many opportunities for a strategic sale, as large MNCs and even unicorns in India are always on the lookout for entities which fill white spaces in their offerings.

✓ Strategic sale is a much faster path to wealth creation than an IPO.

✓ If you have consistently created value, odds are that a buyer will beat a path to your door probably through an intermediary, like an investment banker. You may also consider giving a mandate for sale of the business.

✓ When you sell your venture, price and valuation should not be the only consideration. Look also for an organization that will provide the best home for your team.

✓ The standard rules for enterprise valuation do not apply to a strategic sale. The valuation should be based on what the acquirer can achieve with the acquisition and the strategic objectives it fulfils for the acquirer. The keys to a good price are the IPs and capabilities you have built, and the future-proofing of your platform/product. It's good to aim for the moon in a strategic sale.

✓ Odds are when you sell your venture, the CEO and some senior members of the team will find no place in the acquired entity after a transition period. It's best to start planning your new future in parallel, unless you do get a challenging role in the new set-up.

10.

Your Initial Public Offering

'The idea of waiting for something makes it more exciting'

—Andy Warhol

There are many ups and downs, joys and tribulations in the life of an entrepreneur. The joys include securing your first customer, raising your first invoice, registering your first million dollars of profit and the joy of your initial public offering (IPO).

According to Ashok, nothing is more exciting and exhilarating than being in the stock exchange with your co-founders, ringing the bell to mark the commencement of trading and to watch your share price register a steadily increasing trend. Ever since you implemented your idea, most of you have worked towards this moment. This is the end of a journey as a private limited company and the beginning of a new one as a publicly traded company. You will acquire a new set of investors to whom you will be accountable. For the first time, you will not have to worry about providing an exit to your investors. The market will provide them with their entries and exits. To ensure that your IPO is indeed an invigorating and not a disappointing event requires a lot of advance planning, detailed work and patience for the right time to enter the market and execute your IPO.

In this chapter, we will cover the preparations you need to make for your IPO, as well as assessing your readiness for the IPO, sizing the issue, pricing and valuation of your company, choosing the stock exchange on which to list and managing the issue process. We will also cover a few of the key issues on running a public company to sensitize you to regulatory issues so that you don't inadvertently become non-compliant or violate the law.

Preparing for Your IPO

If you began your entrepreneurial journey with the intent of going public, you should have started preparing for it right from the formation of your company. We have covered some of the governance requirements in the chapter on 'Building Your Organization'. Even if you are ultimately seeking a trade sale, you have to make yourself an attractive acquisition target and many of the preparations needed for IPO will need to be put into place to prepare your company for a trade sale. Over the years, the governance and audit requirements for even private limited companies have been tightened considerably, so most of what's needed should already be in place.

In the US, as a public company you will come under the purview of the Sarbanes–Oxley (SOX) Act and need to be aware of all the stipulations, including penal provisions for non-compliance. When this law was enacted, it was considered onerous and many companies even hesitated to list in the US because of the overheads for compliance. Now, even in India, with Section 49 of the listing rules set by the SEBI and the New Companies Act, we have caught up with much of global standards for stringent requirements. There are some sections of the Companies Act which are not applicable to private limited companies. At Happiest Minds, we have tried to ensure compliance wherever possible with the entire act even prior to going public. You will be well advised to look into all clauses which become applicable at IPO and develop early the necessary systems and processes to comply. This exercise is not trivial and you should begin this effort about eighteen months prior to going public.

This is also a good time to revisit all your policies and see if policies like whistle-blower, sexual harassment and non-discrimination are in place and incorporate the best practices. Certain philosophies also need to be articulated. For example, if your approach on compensation is to be in the second quartile of your industry, you need to articulate this clearly and ensure that your actual position conforms to the stated position. The guiding principle behind all such policies and disclosures is that the new investors and industry analysts will want an outside-in view of the company, which is derived from the inside-out view you provide. Outside investors need to have confidence that everything is open and transparent and what you see is what you get. According to prescriptive guidelines, you will need to segment your market in different ways and report your performance along these lines. At Happiest Minds, we already slice and dice our data in many ways. It is our intent to put all such information in the open domain when we go public, though we know that most public companies in our industry don't reveal as much, with a view to limiting access to competitive information.

All of the above—including capture and presentation of historical data on value drivers, audit trails and taxation—become part of the building blocks for your IPO. Your goal should be to benchmark against the best in the world on transparency and governance.

Expanding and Reconstituting Your Board of Directors

About a year prior to the IPO you will need to expand your board. In a company with an executive chairman, 50 per cent of the board members must be independent directors (33 per cent if there is a non-executive chairman who is also an independent director). Up until now, the VCs, while safeguarding their investments, also safeguarded the company. In a public company, investors are not considered independent directors who safeguard the interests of minority shareholders.

For a company which has two VCs on the board and two management representatives, you will now need a minimum board size of eight, representing an addition of four independent directors. We would advise that the board size be limited to eight until the company becomes much larger, as a board has its own overheads and manageability issues. The next issue is: what should be the profile of the new board members? In his MindTree days, Ashok created a high-profile and prestigious board, which also meant a very expensive board considering that MindTree was only worth about $120 million at the time the board was expanded. At that time, V.G. Siddhartha, as a VC and board member, asked Ashok whether such an expensive board was worthwhile. In hindsight, Ashok agrees with Siddhartha and for Happiest Minds, he intends to take a different approach. Ashok explains his views in his words and also contrasts the value addition from the independent directors at MindTree with the value derived through the advisory board at Happiest Minds which, as mentioned earlier, is a no-fee board:

> About eighteen months before MindTree's proposed listing, I began the search for our new board members. I had to look out for six additions as we had two VC

representatives and four internal board members. Through my personal network and introductions from friends, it was not long before I had six acceptances from individuals of four different nationalities and all big names: a European who headed a multibillion-dollar MNC, a professor from one of the most prestigious academic institutes in the world, a person who had served on the technology advisory committee of President Bush, a diplomat who had decided to quit his country's diplomatic service and develop an alternate career in India, a retired CEO serving on many boards and a retired bureaucrat who had contributed enormously to the Indian IT industry's development and was also a role model for corporate governance.

So why do I agree with Siddhartha who, even now, sometimes gently reminds me that he had cautioned against this high-profile board? When I look back, the one thing that jumps out in my memory is that not one of the board members even questioned the wisdom of our entering the phone business (as discussed earlier, the accountability for the decision was entirely mine). Also, I can't remember a single important strategic change which originated from the board meetings. Maybe it was my own fault in not getting the best out of the board as no one could doubt their pedigree and experience. Also, I had selected the board members without clarity on what I expected from the board. It was more a trophy-hunter approach of getting big names and the impression of prestige and prominence. Other than the ex-government officer, Mr Vittal, who had contributed so much towards the growth of the industry, none of the board members understood the IT services industry. In contrast, the advisory board at Happiest Minds comprises global CIOs who in every meeting throw up multiple new ideas—and ideas are priceless.

In light of the above experience at MindTree, Ashok would seek the following profiles as independent directors on his Happiest Minds board: one finance expert (Gopalan already being in place), one people-practice specialist, and two members who know the IT services industry well either as strategists, functional experts or end users.

Finally, apart from looking at the professional qualifications of the board members, do also look at them as individuals and try to assess how well they will gel with each other and align to the company's mission, vision and values. Discreet reference checks are in order as even a single dysfunctional board member can ruin the atmosphere, hamper productivity and make board meetings a less gratifying experience for the others.

Once your new board is created, you will need to expand the number of board committees. In addition to the internal audit committee and compensation committee, which you probably already have, you will need to add a shareholders' grievance committee. After twelve months, you should also institute a formal board member evaluation process—which Ashok shied away from in MindTree as it felt a bit embarrassing to evaluate such a high-profile board.

At the end of the day, the acid test of the value of the board members individually and collectively is whether they contribute to making a positive change to the organization. You should look back on your decisions and assess which ones happened because the board influenced the management with cogent arguments and different perspectives. If the board merely endorses management recommendations or marginally tweaks them, it's not good enough. This is

Ashok's primary expectation from the board of his next public company.

How Ready Are You for a Public Issue?

Your readiness for a public issue is equally a function of your past track record and the visibility of your future performance. The basic parameters for both past and future assessments are revenue and profit growth, together with balance sheet ratios like return on equity (RoE) and return on capital employed (RoCE). Future potential value drivers such as new market segments or new products or services should be clearly discernible. If you need to implement a pivoting strategy, an IPO is not the right place to go; instead you should go to another VC or PE player for additional funding.

The objectives for which you are raising money should make clear business sense, whether it is capacity expansion, acquisitions or other aspects. You should have appointed merchant bankers who are confident of successfully taking you to market. The role of merchant bankers is discussed in greater detail in the next section.

Finally, even after you are preparing for the issue and there is market awareness that you are planning to go public, financial markets may turn significantly southwards due to a variety of negative events in the national or global political and economic environments. In such situations, there is no shame in deferring the issue and waiting for the next upward cycle, which will typically arrive in the next two to three years. Your merchant bankers are your best advisors in such a situation and if they can still promise you a good response, you can go ahead. However, reconsidering the timing of the issue is okay only for external reasons outside your control. If your business projections begin to look shaky, you may still have to defer the issue, but your credibility will get severely affected.

Selecting Merchant Bankers, Sizing and Pricing the Issue

Well before the time you are gearing up for your IPO, odds are that some investment banking firms would have called on you. They like to visit potential IPO firms about two years before the IPO date with a view to 'building relationships', as they describe it, but in reality to position themselves as your preferred choice. There is quite a wide choice of investment banking entities in the market. Some of them are divisions of large MNCs or Indian banks; several others are stand-alone entities whose prime focus is investment banking. All of them will show you the standard league tables of successful IPOs, demonstrating they are the biggest or the best. Though there is competition in the industry, they seldom compete on the basis of price and you should expect to spend about 4 per cent of the money raised in the Indian market, of which the fees to bankers will range from 1.25 per cent to 3 per cent, depending on the size of the issue. About 25 per cent of the fee can be made a variable success fee.

You may find the credentials of many of the bankers satisfactory and the difference comes from the team that will work on your account. Don't make your decision based on meetings with the managing director or a suave sales head. For a few shortlisted bankers, ask to see the actual team which will work on your IPO project. You should grill the team in detail as you would a candidate you are selecting to hire. Ascertain the level of their relationships when they take you on investor roadshows, and get firm commitments on the quantity and quality of meetings they will seek. A typical issue will require a hundred-plus meetings spread across Singapore, Hong Kong, the US, the UK and India. Examine the presentation packages they have created for past customers as well as the documentation, such as the prospectus. Get a feel of the team's enthusiasm for your listing and their confidence in making it a success. You should select two or more investment bankers based on the size of the issue. One of them will become the lead manager for the issue and take responsibility for the prospectus and all statutory filings and will be paid a fixed sum in the region of Rs 50–75 lakh, in addition to the fees for marketing the IPO.

One of the first things you have to decide with your merchant banker is the size of your issue. The starting point has to be very clear, i.e. the objectives for which you are raising funds: capacity expansion, for developing new products or services, for acquisition and so on. While stating your planned use of funds in the prospectus, it's important to broad-base the requirements as funds raised cannot be used for reasons other than those stated. You should also be sure that the funds raised will be adequate for at least three years as you can't go back to the market repeatedly or on short notice. Another aspect is one of control and not diluting equity beyond what is essential. Indian law, unlike the US, specifies a minimum of 25 per cent share for new shareholders on going public. Accordingly, if the founders hold 50 per cent of the company pre-IPO, this will come down to 37.5 per cent despite minimum dilution. If some of the existing investors want to use the IPO to exit all or part of their holdings, this will increase the size of the issue, though this additional amount, known as the secondary offering, doesn't come into the company. The secondary offering does help the founders with lower dilution as new investors get 25 per cent, but existing non-founders go down or out. Once you determine the desired size of the issue through the above process, you should discuss it with your investment banker who will help you fine-tune the amount. In a booming market, the banker may suggest you raise a larger amount on the principle that equity should be raised when you can and not when you need it. They may also insert a green shoe option, which is an option to increase the offering by an agreed per cent in the event of oversubscription.

Incidentally, in 2015, the average size of an issue in the Indian market was about Rs 350 crore (about $50 million), excluding the top five giant issues above Rs 1000 crore. This number is an average, but anything below Rs 200 crore for an issue would be too small.

The final piece of the IPO-planning puzzle is the price of the IPO. If there are comparables in the market, their forward P/E ratios will give an indicator of the price which should be set. A young company with higher growth rates may be able to attract funding at a premium over comparables. There is also what we call good corporate governance premium. MindTree benefited enormously from this and Ashok expects that so will Happiest Minds when the time comes for its IPO. Once you have the issue size and price, you know the market capitalization at which your company will be making its debut on the market.

Price discovery of an issue can be done through two different methods: the book-building approach and the fixed-price approach. Companies tend to enter with a fixed price in mind, but go through price discovery by book-building which factors in supply and demand. We leave it to you to understand the technicalities of these two approaches as also the rules regarding underwriting from your merchant banker who will also advise you regarding the preferred methodology for your issue.

In spite of so many experienced minds who are engaged in the process of sizing and pricing the issue, it is surprising to find a very high proportion, close to 50 per cent, of issues trading below issue price two to three years after IPO. This phenomenon is elegantly explained by Anup Bagchi, CEO & MD of ICICI Securities, who feels that the process of pricing and valuation is not addressed holistically at the IPO stage. According to Anup, valuation is an independent vector settled largely on the basis of market multiples of earnings per share (EPS), but it is in reality an intersection of your unfolding story and maths. The market also has an expectation of future compounded average growth rate (CAGR) and valuation does have a correlation to this CAGR number. On the other hand, pricing is a momentum game. Another tenet is that an IPO is a bull-market phenomenon. People want to enter the market when there is a positive hump. Furthermore, existing investors tend to push for a price which maximizes their gains, particularly if they are using the IPO to exit. Given these push factors, it's not surprising that many issues find themselves in negative territory. Also, Anup says, companies sometimes confuse high oversubscription with the success of an issue. He feels that an optimum oversubscription is ten to twelve times the issue size. Anything above that indicates undervaluation and something below that portends a lack of follow-on demand.

Choosing Your Stock Exchange

When choosing the stock exchange to list on, the first thing to decide is if you prefer doing a listing abroad or a listing in your own market. The Indian stock market was dull for several years so many companies with high-value issues chose to list abroad. As a consequence, the SEBI has liberalized rules to make issuance in India easier and more effective whereby the new issue market has picked up.

For an overseas listing, the UK was popular in the past for Indian companies but listing there has now slowed to a trickle. The largest listing market in the world has become China, but it seems unlikely to be an attractive destination for Indian companies. There is the odd deal in Singapore. This leaves the

US as the de facto only real choice for an overseas listing if you are not going to list in your own market.

If you want to list in the US, ideally you should have planned for this from inception and registered your company in the US. However, if you, as the India-based entrepreneur, also want to put in significant money to increase your shareholding, you would have had to limit this in line with what the Reserve Bank of India allows for such overseas investments. For example, this option would not have been available at Happiest Minds, as Ashok is the largest investor and would not have been able to remit the required amount to the US. Even if you have not registered your company in the US, you can still list there by converting your company into a US-registered company. However, this is a tedious process and we would not recommend diverging time and energy that is better devoted to building your business.

The major advantage of a US listing is the premium over the Indian market, particularly for technology companies listing on the NASDAQ. The premium can vary between 15–30 per cent. Even though the cost of the issue in the US is about 7 per cent—against 4 per cent in India—the higher share price premium makes the effective cost of capital in the US lower and you will have lower dilution for the same amount raised in India. Another advantage of a US listing is that you can take even a loss-making company to the market as they are willing to take a long-term view for sunrise industries instead of basing the price on revenue or EBIDTA multiples. In India also, the rules have been relaxed to allow listings of loss-making companies on smaller exchanges but the efficacies of these have yet to be tested. Operationally, a US listing would be preferred if your major market is the US and if you also employ several people in the US. The US customers will feel greater comfort if they see you as a US company and it will contribute to brand building.

Also, US employees can be given ESOP of the US stocks, which again will be preferred and not impacted by devaluation of the rupee against the dollar.

That said, there are three major disadvantages of listing in the US as compared to India. Firstly, the US is a highly litigious society and you have a higher probability of being at the receiving end of a class action suit by shareholders or a target of activist shareholders. Also, the US SEC tends to be tougher on what the India SEBI may treat as a transgression that merits a cautionary warning. These disadvantages can be articulated as hypotheticals, but it is up to you to run your business in such a manner so as to not become the object of punitive actions.

The third disadvantage of listing in the US, higher vulnerability to a hostile acquisition, is a very real one and can undermine your goal of creating and leading a company. In the US, when the board receives a takeover offer, it has a fiduciary responsibility to consider whether it is in the best interests of the shareholders. As a 2007 Harvard case study by David Millstone and Guhan Subramanian on Oracle vs PeopleSoft observed, in 'hostiles you come in hard, you come in high and you come in once'. There is very little chance of a company even as large and successful as PeopleSoft being able to fend off a hostile bid from an entity as powerful as Oracle. This is a David and Goliath battle with the odds stacked in favour of Goliath. In India, hostile bids have to begin with acquiring a 26 per cent stake in the company through market buying and then making an open offer to all shareholders, but such events are not very common or frequent.

For an Indian company, the first listing has to be in India. If yours is at least a billion-dollar market cap company and you are considering raising at least $150–200 million, you can consider a dual listing. Otherwise, if you are keen on a US listing, you will need to wait for your second visit to the market when you can raise money in the US through an instrument known as an American Depository Receipt (ADR).

Having described so many possible options, we would recommend that you keep things simple and choose to list in India. Between India's two leading stock exchanges, the National Stock Exchange (NSE) provides you greater liquidity, but you may as well list on both the NSE and the Bombay Stock Exchange (BSE). Your aim should be to offset the loss of a US listing premium by getting a good governance premium.

Life after the IPO

After a successful IPO, many things will change for you and your company which will influence your priorities and the way you work. For the first year after the IPO, the CEO may need to spend 20 per cent of his or her bandwidth and the CFO up to 40 per cent for the following new requirements:

- **Accountability to your new shareholders:** The main obligation you have to your new shareholders is that you should give them a fair return on their investments. As a young company, you should have higher growth than a large player and you should be able to deliver appreciation at a minimum share price which is above the average for companies on the stock exchange of your choice. Unfortunately, the SEBI data shows that above 50 per cent of companies that listed in India till 2013 were trading at prices lower than the issue price. Does this indicate that the issue was overpriced in the first instance? Or is it due to the result of these companies falling significantly short of projections promised at IPO?

  There can be company structure-specific reasons. Café Coffee Day is one such company whose shares declined almost 20 per cent shortly after going public, even the though results seemed to be in line with projections. The reason here, according to V.G. Siddhartha, is that they took the holding company public and the Indian market in general does not like a holding company structure. If this is truly the reason, we would say that it is still a case of overpricing the issue as the investment bankers should have advised Siddhartha of this market feature and recommended a lower issue price or recommended taking the operating (rather than the holding) company Café Coffee Day public.

Sometimes it will be noted that share prices start shooting up because of irrational exuberance in the market or some company-specific rumours not founded on fact. When this happens, it is the retail investor who gets hurt most as he or she doesn't realize that entry is taking place at the peak of the wave. When this sharp, northward movement transpired in the MindTree shares shortly after listing, Ashok went on-air on CNBC to state that the fundamentals had not changed since the IPO. This unusual move was highly appreciated by CNBC's impeccable lead anchor, Udayan Mukherjee, and it led to a stabilizing of the share price rather than a hard landing of the price, which would have followed had the shares continued with their steep, upward climb.

- **Investor and analyst relations cell:** Once you go public, you will be in the cross-hairs of the analysts in the industry. Likewise, there will be multiple issues or information requests from investors that will constantly need addressing. It is imperative to set up a cell which can service both needs to conserve costs.

People manning these cells should understand that transparency is important, but they also need to be clear on what is appropriate for disclosure, and that no forward-looking statements should be made other than those formally qualified or disclosed as forward-looking statements in board meetings or otherwise. An issue you'll have to settle is whether or not to provide guidance to investors/analysts on results and, if so, whether this should be on a quarterly or annual basis. Our current thinking is to avoid specific numbers, but to guide investors on the basis of broad statements such as, 'We expect our growth to be above the industry average or in the top XYZ per cent of the industry.' If you decide to provide guidance and the business becomes very unpredictable, you should discontinue the guidance till normalcy returns. Whether you provide guidance or not, the analysts will publish their expectations and your share price will respond to not only your absolute numbers, but also to whether you have exceeded, met or been below the average of analyst expectations.

One overriding principle in dealing with external communications once you go public is to be proactive about communicating bad news, be it to analysts or to the stock exchange.

- **Education regarding quiet periods and insider trading:** Instruction is important not only for the founders and the CFO, but a group designated as the leadership team in the company. A company needs to define what its quiet period is, which can be wider but not narrower than what is prescribed by the SEBI. During this period, the leadership team shall not make any public statements regarding the business or expected results of the company. Likewise, they will not do any trading of the company's shares. Leaders also have constraints on trading which go beyond the quiet period, which come into being whenever they are in possession of market-sensitive information that is not public knowledge. This could include a committed acquisition, the impending transition of a senior person like the CEO, or any major inflection anticipated in the business. Leaders should also not share such information with anyone who may take advantage of it, to avoid finding themselves accused of leaking insider information, as it happened with Rajat Gupta. The CFO should alert the leader about quiet periods and non-trading periods, as our experience shows that most violations occur inadvertently due to lack of awareness.

- **Avoiding short-term orientation:** A big negative of analyst and market scrutiny is to introduce a short-term orientation in management, focused on delivering quarterly results. We would strongly advise that you keep your focus on your five-year vision and goals and plan your actions accordingly. While being sensitive to short-term share price dips, don't become paranoid about them. Above all, listen to analyst comments but don't let them dictate to you what and how you will do on strategic matters having medium- and long-term impact. These decisions are the prerogative and responsibility of you and your board.

Ashok has, so far, experienced the joy of one successful IPO at MindTree. He looks forward to another happy experience in the future for Happiest Minds. Gopalan too has witnessed with pride many of the companies he has mentored or advised make the transition from being start-ups to publicly traded entities.

We hope that this book has provided you with many takeaways that will contribute towards a successful IPO.

Success can mean different things to different people. We believe that a successful IPO is one which gives fair returns to both existing investors and a healthy appreciation for new investors. The extent of oversubscription and the like are only noise factors. To be more precise:

- For existing investors, the appreciation should be 4x or 5x and upwards on their entry price or an IRR which is comparable with the top few companies that have gone public in your space.
- For new investors, we define a successful IPO as one which, over a three-year period, gives new investors a minimum of 10 per cent higher returns than the average of comparables or your industry average.

KEY TAKEAWAYS

✓ The most exciting and exhilarating experience in the life of an entrepreneur is the listing of your IPO and seeing a steady upward tick in your share price.

✓ An IPO requires years of advance planning. If you put the right governance in place from the beginning, in a sense your preparation for an IPO begins then. In India, you need to become fully compliant with Section 49 of the Companies Act which contains clauses not applicable to private limited companies. If you are listing in the US, you need to ensure compliance with the Sarbanes–Oxley (SOX) Act.

✓ In an IPO, your new investors and industry analysts will seek an outside view of your company based on the inside-out view you provide. It is recommended to take an approach of best-in-class disclosure and transparency. This covers both historical data on your company, segmentation of your business and defining your current and future value drivers.

✓ About twelve to eighteen months before the IPO, you should expand and reconstitute your board. A company with an executive chairman is required to have 50 per cent independent directors, otherwise 33 per cent. We recommend a maximum of eight members on the board till you become a much larger company.

✓ You need to be clear on your expectations from the board and select the members accordingly. It is essential to have one independent director with a finance background who also becomes the chairman of the audit committee. We would recommend that instead of packing your board with prestigious names you bring in persons with complementary functional capabilities (say a people or marketing expert) and persons who understand your industry. The latter are very useful in making strategic decisions.

✓ Once the new board is in place, you will need to add board committees which you did not require while still a private limited company. These will include a shareholders' grievance committee and a nominations committee. A formal board member evaluation process should also be enabled. The value you derive from the board should be assessed by asking what your company would or would not have done but for the board's interventions. Discreet reference checks before you appoint a board member are also in order as a single dysfunctional member can reduce productivity and make the board experience a less gratifying one.

✓ The most important step for planning and implementing your IPO is to appoint two or more merchant bankers who will help you to size your issue, price the issue, package the offering and promote the issue through roadshows etc. Most investment bankers come with impressive credentials. Before you select your merchant bankers, ask to meet with the specific team that will work on your issue. Assess the strength of their relationships, get commitments on the meetings they will seek out for you during roadshows and also assess their enthusiasm for your issue. The bankers will also assess your readiness for an IPO. During the course of IPO preparation, if markets take a deep downward dip, there is no shame in deferring the launch of your issue.

✓ For determining the size of the issue, you need to be very clear on the objectives for which you are raising money. For example, is it capacity expansion, creating a war chest for acquisition, or an exit path for your initial investors—or a combination of all these?

✓ The price will be derived from your industry comparables, your growth rate and profitability etc. You can also expect a premium for good governance.

✓ In spite of so many experienced minds who work on your IPO's pricing and valuation, many new issues tend to trade below issue price two to three years after the IPO. This is because an IPO is a momentum event which usually occurs on a hump of the market. Also, existing investors tend to push for maximum returns particularly if they are exiting.

✓ One of the most important decisions you must take is whether you want to list your company in the US (or any other country) or your home base in India. Unless you have planned for the US at inception by registering your company in the US, we would recommend you go with the simpler option of your home base.

✓ The major advantage of listing in the US is that the cost of capital is lower as you can get a significant share price premium. Also, for sunrise industries, the US market gives good valuations based on growth potential even for loss-making companies. A US listing also gives you a brand boost and is advantageous if the US is your major market. US-based employees would also prefer ESOPs of a US company.

✓ The major disadvantages of a US listing is that it is a more litigious culture, your cost of compliance will be higher and a public company in the US is more vulnerable to hostile acquisition than a company in India. While the US market can give your share price a premium, it will also punish you harder if your company's performance is below expectations. The price premium in the US market can be offset by a good governance premium in India.

✓ Life post-IPO will place you under increased scrutiny. The CEO and CFO will have to spare a significant proportion of their bandwidth for at least twelve months. You should set up investor and analyst relationship cells. One principle for transparency is to be proactive in communicating bad news. The increased scrutiny should not lead you to develop a short-term orientation driven by the need to achieve quarterly results. Never lose sight of your vision and base your strategic decisions on achieving the same. Educate your team so that leaders do not inadvertently trip up during quiet periods and insider trading guidelines.

✓ We believe this book contains many takeaways which will help you to execute a successful IPO. For those of you who choose not to take the IPO path, these takeaways will also help you to create a successful company and fashion it as an attractive candidate for acquisition.

✓ We define a successful IPO as one which gives existing investors a 4x to 5x and upwards return on the entry price and new investors a minimum of 10 per cent higher returns than the average of your industry in a three-year period.

11.

Failure and Success: Two Ends of a Spectrum

'Failure should be our teacher, not our undertaker. Failure is delay, not defeat. It is a temporary detour, not a dead end'

—Denis Waitley

'Everyone who achieves success in a venture, solves each problem as they came to it. They helped themselves. And they were helped through powers known and unknown to them at the time they set out on their voyage'

—W. Clement Stone

All of *Entrepreneurship Simplified* is about assisting you, the entrepreneur, in improving your probability of success and reducing your probability of failure. In this final chapter, we don't intend to condense or revisit all of what we have written, but will share a few overviews and perspectives.

Before we proceed, let's articulate what we define as success and failure in the context of your venture. A lot of the literature on entrepreneurship will give you a laundry list of actions, or lack thereof, which lead to failure. To us, many of these actions are just mistakes, a few of which are inevitable in the course of building a business. Ashok can think of at least five mistakes which cost $500,000 each in his MindTree days. (This doesn't include the decision to enter the smartphone business, which led to an $8 million loss, but at least it was set off by the service revenues from the Kyocera acquisition.) Such mistakes are not failures, at least not in the broad context of your whole venture. Ashok sees these mistakes as the cost of building a billion-dollar market cap company where many things were done well and several others could have been done better. These included a few errors of judgement, be it on people, markets or technologies.

When we talk about the failure of a venture, we define it as:

- Pulling down the shutters, letting go of the team. Literally shutting shop.
- Doing a distress sale at a throwaway price.
- Doing a down-round which effectively wipes out existing shareholder value.

In the last definition above, the new shareholders could very well revive the venture and make it a success. However, the founders and the venture are dead for all practical purposes as they will get no value, as happened in the case of Bloodhound in the US. We hasten to add that if you find yourself in this difficult situation, it is only the end of a venture and a prelude to the beginning of the next phase of your life. Take heart from none other than Vinod Khosla who says, 'I have failed more times than I have succeeded in all the things I have tried. It is just that every time I failed, I did not give up trying new things—that is what made me successful.'

Having defined failure and success as the two ends of a spectrum, a failure along the lines of shutting shop or a distress sale will get a score of 1 or 2 on a scale of 10.

What is the definition of success? In our IPO chapter, we have defined a successful IPO as one which gives attractive returns to existing and also new investors in a three-year cycle post-IPO. But a successful venture is more than just one which gives a good financial ROI, whether through an IPO or a strategic sale. A successful venture must also involve the creation of an institution which is built on the foundation of good governance and a committed team to sustain the success. We typically measure such success in a seven- to ten-year time frame as it takes that much time to build an institution. On this criterion, Happiest Minds is still a work in progress and, hopefully, a success in the making.

Completing our perspective on failure and success as two ends of a spectrum, scores from 3 to 5 will represent varying degrees of underperformance with 3 representing a high danger of future failure. Scores of 6 to 8 would be good going in a challenging world. We would reserve 9 and 10 for companies that have built a base to be successful for twenty years or more. There is no formula or hard-and-fast rules for our scoring system. We just leave this as a tool for your own self-assessment of success. As an indicator, we would put MindTree, Titan Industries and Yes Bank in the 6 to 8 bracket while Infosys, Airtel, Google, Microsoft and Facebook as successes in the 9 to 10 bracket. Of course, during the life journey of an enterprise, there is nothing to prevent a 6–8 scale company from moving to the upper end.

Timing Is Everything

You may have noticed a recurring thread as you went through *Entrepreneurship Simplified*, i.e. the importance of timing in virtually everything you do as you build your venture. This starts as early as idea selection to entry in the market. Sometimes the idea is way ahead of its time, perhaps because the market doesn't have a need for the product/service or it just could be that the supporting technology infrastructure is not ready. For example, most current virtual businesses would not be successful without the availability of inexpensive broadband and mobile technologies. Many of the failed dot-coms didn't take off because the communication infrastructure of the late 1990s was inadequate to provide a rich, real-time customer experience to sustain demand. Companies like Fab Mall, India Plaza and Rediff shopping failed because the Internet penetration in India was very low to support adequate demand. A decade later their successor companies are doing exceedingly well.

Several other ventures fail because they enter the market too late. When a segment is seen as 'hot', everyone wants to rush in to grab a slice of the opportunity. Even VCs can succumb to this tendency to follow the herd in spite of several ventures having already entered the space. Such an attitude leads to an overcrowding of the opportunity and many failures. This happened to the non-banking financial services industry in the late 1980s and early 1990s—many new entrants had to shut down.

Curiously, out of the twin dangers of being too early or too late, the former is the bigger hazard. If there is no obvious need in the market, a start-up can't easily generate or create that demand. Here the market will need a large player with deep pockets. If you are a late entrant, you still have a chance of gaining a share of the market by exploiting the weaknesses of existing players, creating differentiating strategies and employing approaches like judo strategy and Tai Chi thinking.

For product companies, the time to market and time to revenue are critical factors for success. Timing also comes into play when you raise funds and later, when you do your IPO as you want to strategize both on the back of resurgent financial markets.

Strangely enough, your business launch can be effective even when markets are slow or in recession. Some of the greatest companies in the world, including Microsoft and Cisco, were born in recessionary conditions. The reasoning for their long-term success is that if you can succeed in tough times, you will prosper further when the good times arrive. Conversely, companies launched in a boom period may get euphoric, over expand, burn up too much cash and get trapped when the downturn comes, which was what happened when the dot-com bust came. We are, of course, not advocating that you wait for a recessionary time to launch, but you needn't hold back your entry plans for such reasons. The optimum approach is to catch the groundswell of booming demand and be cautious about your spends. As Ashok says, use the good times to prepare for the bad, as the down cycle will inevitably follow.

Moreover, timing is important in terms of your approach to scaling up. Too early and you will have poorly utilized assets and higher cash burn than the market can justify. Too late and someone else will grab your market and the investment you have already made will be threatened. The timing of people addition has to precede the opportunity you want to address on the earlier articulated principle of building ahead of time the organization you want to be.

Timing is further critical in implementing a pivoting strategy if the need arises. Too early and you may be abandoning your idea before giving it a fair chance. Too late and you may find you have literally run out of time—with not enough cash to execute the strategy, no investor support and the loss of key talent.

Timing is also important when it comes to acquisition. We believe too many start-ups do acquisitions too soon, before they have moulded their own unique culture. Also, start-up stage money is your most expensive and it should be used to develop your core value proposition rather than buying something you can ill afford to do. How many times have we seen high-profile start-ups make acquisitions and just a little later, be forced to do layoffs due to shortage of funds? Zomato is one such recent example.

Ashok used to tell audiences during his talks that a CEO, particularly a start-up CEO, needs to be like the conductor of a symphony, to ensure that all parts of the company are in tune and the timing of all major decisions is right. He now realizes that the start-up CEO's job is much tougher. The conductor is well versed in the music to follow; the players of the orchestra are also well versed in what is expected of them and when. An entrepreneur–CEO has to ensure everything works smoothly in the face of huge uncertainties. Are there any guidelines we can give to help the entrepreneur accurately size up the timing of action and decisions? While implementation is outside the purview of this book, we do say that always ask yourself if this is the right time for any major programme you are launching. For decision-making, we would recommend Ashok's 'head, heart and gut' approach.

What Is the Role of Luck in Success and Failure?

Not just successful entrepreneurs but VCs too will say that luck has played a large part in their success. Deepak Kamra of Canaan is forthright in saying that luck has played a very large part in the bets he made and the success of the ventures in which he has invested. He does add though that you have to get yourself into a position where luck does happen. Vinod Khosla is quoted in a cover story of the *Smart Techie* in December 2011 as saying that out of the ten or so factors that contribute to an entrepreneur's success, three or four are controlled by the competition, three or four by you (the entrepreneur), and the rest is luck. Ashok recalls the luck factor from his MindTree days as well, when the money for the second round of funding was credited into the bank account one week before 9/11 happened. But for this fortuitous timing of getting the money just before the major tragedy hit the US and the world, MindTree could well have joined the dust heap of failed companies that collapsed with the dot-com bust. Many other entrepreneurs modestly attribute their success to good luck. As in life so also in entrepreneurship, good luck does play a part, but the key thing is that the ostensibly lucky entrepreneurs contribute to their own luck by being in the right place at the right time and grabbing the right opportunity. Also, luck cannot explain the repeated successes of serial entrepreneurs like K. Ganesh.

So if good luck does contribute partially to success, is the converse also true? Does bad luck contribute to failure or are some failures primarily due to bad luck? We believe that is not the case. It is the job of the entrepreneur to be prepared for one of several possible negative events and have contingency plans ready for implementation. Otherwise, it could be argued that bad luck is the reason hundreds of dot-com companies and 98 per cent of e-business integrators collapsed when the bubble burst, while the real reason is that most of these companies were carried away by the hype that accompanied the dot-com boom. Many of them over expanded, few of them conserved their cash. The euphoric feedback made them overconfident to the extent that you could say they were guilty of drinking their own Kool-Aid.

So instead, what is commonly called bad luck is what we label as not recalibrating your assumptions and the inability to see change coming. Ed Rogers of NASA, whom Ashok considers one of the clearest thinkers he has met, explains why people don't see change coming. He says, 'You have to detect a wave from the ocean floor, not when you see it at the top. You don't see it because you don't know what to look for and where to look for it.' Another perspective on 'bad luck' contributing to failure is missing early warning signs and thereby failing to act in time.

Most Frequent Causes for Failure

Our objective in this section is to look at the conditions for success and see how to replicate them. However, since a high percentage of start-ups fail, it is perhaps more prudent to first look at the major reasons for failure.

We classify failed ventures into two groups: the first is linked with personal reasons or characteristics, and the second are business reasons.

Up till now in this book we have not questioned whether you yourself, as the entrepreneur, are ready for entrepreneurship. We have said that you are ready when you feel it's the right time and you see the right opportunity. The truth is that entrepreneurship is not everybody's cup of tea. Thanks to the few very visible, huge successes, entrepreneurship is seen as glamorous and a means to generate enormous wealth and be your own boss. Potential entrepreneurs don't realize that even successful entrepreneurship is preceded by years of sacrifice. By its very nature, entrepreneurship is a ride which provides high highs and low lows. Many people just don't have the stomach and temperament for it. Also, some people are brittle and question the entrepreneurial decision when obstacles occur. Ashok remembers his early MindTree days when there was a threat of legal action from Wipro and also the US founders rejected many members of the India-based team. One of the founders approached him and said it would be better to close down the operation, since the birth of the company had been inaugurated by so much conflict!

Another personal reason for venture failure is often listed as founder conflict and inability to attract talent. You will recollect that we have defined failure as a drop-dead event. We feel that while founder conflict may lead to underperformance and an unhealthy grapevine for a while, it is unlikely to lead to complete failure. In most cases, one or more founders will decide to come out or be evicted. The earth may shake, but soon a new leadership structure will emerge to help the business move ahead. Such a parting is far better than ongoing conflict.

A lot of other studies indicate the inability to attract talent or not having the right team on board as a vital reason for failure. In this knowledge era, if you can't attract talent, you will be in deep trouble. But if you can't attract talent, you should not have veered into entrepreneurship in the first place. In a talent-constrained world, odds are that you will have talent gaps, and you will get a mix of A and B players instead of your preference for an all A-team. Such talent-related issues and how successfully you handle them well influence your performance, but not lead to 'shutters down' failure.

Let's come now to the business reasons for failure. A study by CB Insights in October 2014 on the top twenty reasons why start-ups fail lists the top two reasons as 'no market need' and 'ran out of cash'. We identify these as the root-cause reasons for shutting-down failures. The other reasons are either subsets of these or mistakes which can affect performance but not necessarily cause closure of the venture. Under 'no market need', we would include mistakes like going to market too early, inadequate or misleading market research, wrong product or service development and a flawed business model.

Running out of cash is usually the final manifestation and the trigger for pulling down shutters. However, it includes a host of other mistakes: underestimating the time to revenue, spending ahead of cash availability, over-leveraging, draining out your cash due to acquisitions, among others.

Another reason noted by the CB Insights research is 'legal challenges'. Many of these can be overcome as we highlight later in the Happiest Minds and MySQL cases. However, getting caught in lawsuits can also bring down a start-up. Take, for example, the issue raised in some countries on whether Uber drivers are contractors or employees. A company the size of Uber can overcome this, but a smaller company in the same space could succumb to getting an adverse judgement. The threat of complete failure leading to shut down is much more likely in the US than in India. The reasons are threefold: the US is a more litigious society and the costs of legal defence are an order of magnitude higher; also, in India, the time frames for case closure and judgements stretches out almost indefinitely, giving you time to rectify a breach, if any.

One area leading to complete closure not mentioned in the CB Insights study is poor corporate governance. For those indulging in deviant behaviour, venture death can be sudden, even for large organizations as was seen globally for Enron and locally for Kingfisher Airlines.

Before we close this section, we would like to comment on a phenomenon called 'fail fast'. Many writers tend to indicate that if you fail, it's better to do so quickly. Frankly, we are unable to endorse this. We believe that once you have commenced your entrepreneurial journey, you must persevere to survive and eventually flourish. This does not mean that you don't re-strategize or pivot if needed, but you don't give up—at least not till you have explored all avenues and until there are truly no options left. Ultimately, if you do have to shut down, you must have enough cash left to settle your liabilities. This is the honourable way to bow out.

Key Factors for Success

A single huge mistake or the weakest link in your organization can bring about failure. To be on the upper end of our success spectrum, many, many things have to be thought through and implemented well. The important ones amongst these success factors that we have already run through in *Entrepreneurship Simplified* are: idea generation and validation, organization building, fundraising and cash conservation approaches, marketing and brand building. We have talked of a continuum of strategies appropriate for each inflection point in the journey of your venture. We have covered wealth sharing, corporate governance and creating an organizational culture which supports your mission, vision and values. This entire gamut of areas encompasses necessary conditions for success, but even these alone may not be sufficient conditions. We have also discussed the importance of timing and making your own good luck. We urge you to keep on innovating continuously. We alert you to lookout for change in your industry and even as you set out to disrupt existing businesses, ensure you don't suddenly become the disrupted entity.

In addition to the above factors, you and your founding team will need multiple personal attributes to sustain survival, growth and success. These include perseverance, flexibility, agility and resilience, because everything will not work out as you expect. A word which often comes up in books or articles on entrepreneurs is 'passion', specifically, being passionate about your idea. We believe your idea is something in which you need deep conviction, something that you can logically see as a seed which will grow; you don't necessarily need to be passionate or emotionally attached to your idea. If market conditions dictate, you should be prepared to adapt and modify the idea through a pivoting approach or even junk it. Passion is what you demonstrate in the way you work through your commitment, dedication and being a role model to the best of your ability. Here again, we want to put in a cautionary word about passion and some of the personal characteristics mentioned here. We have read many stories of entrepreneurs who get so consumed by their business idea that they work eighteen-hour days and as a result, neglect their personal lives. They may have succeeded in their business, but the question arises: do entrepreneurship and success have to come at a heavy price to your personal life? Fortunately, in the cases of entrepreneurs we have mentored, we have not observed such extremities. There is a major distinction between being passionate and being obsessed, and yet many entrepreneurs unwittingly get trapped in such dysfunctional behaviour. Financial success at such a price in our view is not success at all.

When you think things through carefully, you will see that overly long stints of working hours at a continuous stretch are not needed and are actually counterproductive. Your role as an entrepreneur is to lead a team, delegate and develop others. The quality of your 'thinking' will determine your contribution far more than your acts of 'doing'. Sleepless nights and a tired body don't bring clarity and consistency of thought.

In conclusion, entrepreneurship is a challenging endeavour: there will be many ups and downs and obstacles. It is not the reward at the end of the journey in terms of wealth creation or the IPO which makes it worthwhile. In spite of the sacrifices required, entrepreneurship should be a fun journey, a joyous journey and a journey filled with purpose. Your venture will be truly successful when you achieve financial success—but in a holistic way.

KEY TAKEAWAYS

✓ Failure and success are two ends of a spectrum with shutting shop at one end and an institution built to last twenty years or more at the other.

✓ Failure should not be confused with mistakes, even though the mistakes may collectively cost millions of dollars. Such errors are almost inevitable in the course of building a large business. The only one who makes no mistakes is the one who does nothing.

✓ Failure in the context of a venture is what we grade as 1 or 2 on a scale of 10 in the failure–success spectrum. Grade 1 or 2 failure includes shutting shop and closing the venture, a distress sale or down-round where existing shareholders get next to nothing. But even this type of failure is only a prelude to the beginning of the next phase of your life.

✓ In our failure–success spectrum, scores of 3–5 represent varying degrees of underperformance, with 3 representing a high danger of future failure.

✓ There are no hard-and-fast scoring rules. As an indicator, a score of 6–8 should be assessed by success in a seven to ten years' time frame. Scores of 9–10 are for organizations which have developed the ability to sustain themselves as successful entities in a twenty-year (or beyond) time frame.

✓ A successful venture is not one which only delivers financial returns, but an institution built on the foundation of good governance.

✓ An entrepreneur's effort should be to improve the probability of success and reduce the probability of failure. An ongoing factor for success is to get your timing right, all the way from idea selection, market entry, scale-up timing, pivoting strategy if needed, acquisition etc. You have to strive for the right timing in an environment of uncertainty.

✓ Many successful VCs and entrepreneurs modestly attribute their success to luck. In reality, they contribute significantly to making their own luck by being in the right place at the right time and grabbing the right opportunities.

✓ Failure cannot be explained away as due to bad luck. It is the job of the entrepreneur to be prepared for one of several possible negative events and have contingency plans ready for implementation.

✓ Many failures occur due to a sense of euphoria and hubris from early success. Some others happen due to missing early warning signals and failure to notice impending change—whereby the disruptor become the disrupted.

✓ Failures of ventures can be classified into two broad groups: due to personal reasons or business reasons. Personal reasons include entrepreneurs who just don't have the stomach and temperament for entrepreneurship but realize this only after taking the plunge. A realistic assessment of the sacrifices, stresses and challenges involved is essential before you make the decision to become an entrepreneur.

✓ An external study indicates that the two largest reasons for venture failure are 'no market need' and 'ran out of cash'. Under 'no market need', we would include the mistakes of going to market too early, inadequate or misleading market research, wrong product or service development and a flawed business model. Running out of cash can be traced back to underestimating the time to revenue, overspending, over-leveraging and draining your cash by too-early acquisitions.

- ✓ Legal challenges and lawsuits can sometimes cause venture failure, but mostly these will be time-consuming and costly distractions leading to underperformance for some time.
- ✓ Poor corporate governance can lead to sudden collapse; this can even happen to giant companies.
- ✓ We don't subscribe to a 'fail fast' approach. Once you commence your entrepreneurial journey, you must persevere and do your best to survive and eventually flourish.
- ✓ A single huge mistake can lead to venture failure. To be on the high end of the success spectrum, many, many things have to be done well. This covers the entire gamut of areas covered in this book, from idea generation to the IPO and beyond. All these are necessary but not sufficient conditions for success. In addition, you will need multiple personal attributes like perseverance, flexibility, agility and resilience to support your business.
- ✓ You should be passionate in the way you work as a role model, but don't cross the line and become consumed by your venture. There are too many stories of entrepreneurs who destroyed their personal lives in the process of making their company a success. The success of your venture does not require the price of your or the company's holistic well-being. The quality of your thinking will determine your success, and excessive hours of work or other dysfunctional behaviour will only affect the clarity of your leadership and decision-making.
- ✓ Apart from achieving financial success, entrepreneurship should be a joyous journey and a journey filled with purpose for it to be truly successful.

12.

The Happiest Minds IPO Experience

'I did then what I knew how to do. Now that I know better, I do better'

—Maya Angelou

'All our dreams can come true, if we have the courage to pursue them'

—Walt Disney

'Everybody thinks about the IPO process as a point in time, when they really should be thinking about it as the start of being a public company'

—Mike Nuzzo, CFO, General Nutrition Centers

We listed Happiest Minds on the NSE/BSE on 16 September 2020. It feels like only yesterday that we were experiencing the heady feeling of seeing the issue establish records in terms of oversubscription and listing gains. The oversubscription was 151 times, and the media reported this as the fourth highest in a decade. The share issue price was Rs 166, and it closed the day at Rs 383 for a listing-day gain of 230 per cent, the highest ever in India. We were inundated with messages of congratulations for a 'very successful initial public offering'. I had to remind all my colleagues and myself that the success of an IPO is to be judged not by this immediate market response but by the returns we give to our new shareholders in a three-year period. Accordingly, the IPO is just the beginning of the next phase in the life of Happiest Minds.

Preparing for the Happiest Minds IPO

It's worth checking if we followed the advice in Chapter 10, 'Your Initial Public Offering'. I am happy to report that we completed all that we had suggested in that chapter, which was written four years ago. We expanded our board, bringing in three new independent directors, created policies and transparent data for giving the world an outside–in view. We ran Happiest Minds with all the transparency and high standards of governance expected from a public limited company.

However, the IPO world had changed dramatically since the days of the MindTree IPO, and there were many new experiences and decisions we had to take, as you will see later in this chapter.

Selecting Our Bankers

We decided to speak to four entities before we selected two, whom we saw as having complementary capabilities—one with wide reach and an excellent marketing team, the other with strong conceptual capabilities, which helped us in positioning our IPO well. The parties we chose were I Sec (affiliate of ICICI Bank) and Nomura. Even with the benefit of hindsight I would make the same choice if we had to do it again. While I do endorse both I Sec and Nomura for having met our expectations, I would only caution that what was good for us need not be the best for others. Merchant bankers' organization structures are verticalized, and the key thing is to get confidence in the team, which will handle your IPO. Fortunately, we were able to get one face-to-face session with the full teams of both bankers before the 2020 lockdown started. They both volunteered to bring the actual persons who would handle the issue for us. This was unlike the other bankers whom we did not select. They brought two or three persons, and we found a big gap in their ability to project their capabilities.

One word of caution about the bankers. They have to settle multiple things amongst themselves and tend to squabble over the same. One of them is the 'Banker's Agreement', which I am told always gets settled only at the last moment. I couldn't understand why it hadn't been completed weeks earlier, within a few days of our appointing the bankers. Our chief financial officer (now MD and CFO), Venkatraman, often had to intervene and arbitrate. I would never have the patience to deal with this, and at times I would threaten to intervene and legislate a decision. Luckily, that never became necessary.

The First End-to-End, Digitally Executed IPO in India

We had barely completed our selection of bankers when the COVID clouds began to form. Happiest Minds, appropriately for a 'Born Digital. Born Agile' company, was able to implement 100 per cent work from home, a few days before the lockdown was imposed. There was an inevitable debate whether we should still proceed with our IPO plans. We noticed that globally, stock markets continued to touch new heights or were relatively stable, even while national GDP numbers came crashing down. This showed that markets were willing to discount current year performance to a large extent. Fortunately, the IT services business was holding on well. During the April–June 2020 quarter, we could see ourselves heading for a significant year-over-year and quarterly decline. We could visualize quarterly improvement from the July–September quarter. We were also confident that what we would lose in terms of annual growth would be compensated in the eyes of the market by profit improvement. Thanks to work from home, we were able to negotiate significant rental reductions, travel/immigration costs declined to almost zero, and like the rest of the industry, we decided to avoid increments for the year. Accordingly, we decided without much agonizing to proceed with the IPO. In taking this decision, I must appreciate the support from Avneet Singh, our only director representing investors on the board. JP Morgan had come in through their CMDB II fund and were slated to exit at the IPO. Accordingly, a poor market response on the price front would have hurt them the most. Avneet stood by us, and I am pleased that we were able to justify his faith in us.

Once the decision was made, our finance and legal teams (both internal and external) moved swiftly, and we were able to file the Draft Red Herring Prospectus (DRHP) with SEBI on 10 June 2020.

Marketing the Happiest Minds Issue: USA or Not?

When we did the MindTree IPO, Indian companies were required to list in India first, but dual listing in the US was permissible. At the time of the Happiest Minds IPO, the rules had changed, allowing the first listing to be in the US. However, the regulatory requirements for what is called a Section 144A offering are even more onerous than the increased stringency of the Indian requirements. We also estimated that the issue cost in the US would be almost double that of India. During the MindTree IPO we had noticed that many of the US funds invested through entities in Singapore, Hong Kong or even India. Accordingly, US money was available to support the demand for our IPO. The Indian market also trusted us highly, based on my track record of leading Wipro's IT business and our MindTree record. We, therefore, expected that the price premium we would get in the US would be offset by the corporate governance and market trust premium in India. This, indeed, turned out to be true.

A word of caution for those who, like us, choose not to list in the US. You have a communication embargo with the North American continent during the IPO process and until forty days after listing. This blanket silence includes potential investors, customers and even employees unless they happen to be shareholders. In a way, this hardly matters since in this world of social media all your news is on the Internet all the time. Still, you do have to be cautious. You can speak to *Forbes India*, but speaking to *Forbes*, USA, could cost you a penalty from SEC, USA. The question then arises as to what type of companies should list in the US. There is one category which the US rewards like no other: Companies which are seen as being disruptive of the existing model, and it doesn't matter whether they are still losing tonnes of money and are yet to achieve profitability. The most recent example of such listing is Airbnb, which doubled on listing to touch an astonishing $100 billion market valuation. Its market cap is greater than the sum of Marriott, Hilton and Hyatt. Typical candidates from India could be Byju's, Oyo, Paytm and many of the other unicorns.

Investor Road Shows

Based on requests from our bankers, we did about eighty roadshows, most of them lasting seventy-five-plus minutes against the budgeted sixty minutes. We felt this number of roadshows was excessive. While roadshows are an important part of marketing the issue, we also realized that the bankers need to maintain a relationship with the investors to whom they go back over and over again, whereas we the company will be the banker's customers once or twice in a lifetime.

I cannot overemphasize the importance of the roadshow presentation material and the presenting team. We chose to present with six leaders, far in excess of the standard two or three. The team comprised the three business unit heads: our chief technology officer, chief financial officer and me (Ashok Soota). We felt it was necessary to project our strong team, particularly as there was an impression that Happiest Minds was a one-person-driven company. Also, the range of our services, solutions and technologies required the presence of additional leaders. The presentation was prepared with the help of one of our bankers; and if I may say so, it was an excellent document. The investors loved our positioning of 'Born Digital. Born Agile'. They bought into the comparison we made with three global 100 per cent digital companies, citing them as our true comparators instead of the Indian IT services companies who were on the path of increasing the proportion of their digital businesses. We took the approach of raising upfront the issues which could cause uneasiness. We were able to explain that though we did not have three years of continuous profitability, our numbers—such as RoE, EBITDA per cent and others—spoke for themselves.

We also were able to explain that FY2018, when we'd reported a loss, was a blip, as the two prior years had been profitable. Happiest Minds has an unusual structure of an executive board whose members are individually and collectively the chief executive officer of the company. This comprises the three business unit heads and the CFO. We were able to explain how the executive board was able to turn around the company from its loss in FY2018 and why this structure was effective in many ways, including cross-BU collaboration, decision-making, etc. Finally, and most importantly, considering my age and visibility, we presented our succession plan upfront.

I am now happy to share one major advantage of the virtual world. Due to COVID, we were able to do our roadshows virtually. Most of us were required to speak for only ten minutes at each session. For example, I handled only the first and last slides plus the questions which followed. During the rest of the presentation, I could multitask while on mute and switching off the camera. In my case, I used the spare time to mostly do my yoga, which I would have had to forgo with the morning and afternoon roadshows! My estimate is that the six of us saved 42,000 person-hours combined, apart from the cost and time required for flying into cities like London, Hong Kong, Singapore, Mumbai, Chennai. I am sure that the investors and bankers also gained useful time. I would sincerely recommend that virtual roadshows should become the standard practice in the post-COVID world.

IPO Documentation

Lawyers have now become the centrepiece of the IPO process. Everything has to be drafted by them or cleared by them. We had to engage three legal firms: one lead, another to represent CMDB II (they, of course, had their own lawyers) and international counsel. The most important document in the IPO is the DRHP. My recollection is that in the past this was prepared by our bankers. Now the international counsel was assigned this task. Not surprisingly, they couldn't capture all the nuances of our varied technologies and solutions in their first draft. We then rewrote nearly all of it. And finally, the lawyers edited our work.

What we didn't get right was a strict requirement that anything which could not be proved as factual could not be included. For example, I was not able to write in my résumé that I led the turnaround of Shriram Refrigeration from 1978–84, even though we gave them pre- and post-1978 annual reports. Fortunately, the international counsels did an excellent job in their subsequent deliverables. In summary, I would also express satisfaction with all the three legal companies: Khaitan & Co., Cyril Amarchand, and HSL, Singapore. I do feel, though, that a better way to do the DRHP (excluding the risk section) is to brief management on the dos and don'ts. We prepare the first draft and counsel edits. This could have saved one back-and-forth cycle. It is very important to prepare the DRHP with care, as during the IPO process you are not allowed to make any statements which are not contained in or not consistent with the DRHP. If you include a good industry report made by a reputed organization, you can use their statements which you may not be allowed to make on your own. Although our DRHP was an excellent document, we were to get a surprise, as you will see in the next section.

The IPO Time Schedule and an Unwanted SEBI Surprise

Our bankers listed ninety distinct activities from DRHP filing to listing. Par for the course would be completion in T+90 days, measured from DRHP filing date to listing. I told our bankers, lawyers and team that as an agile company, we should aim for

T+80. This would have meant listing by 8 September. We were well on our way towards achieving the same. SEBI Chennai sent us their first observations to the DRHP on 3 July, and all queries were satisfactorily answered by 8 July except one, which became the googly.

At the time of filing the DRHP, we had asked all our employees who held stock whether they wanted to participate in the offer for sale (OFS) at an indicative price of Rs 155. Not a single one accepted the offer. As a company which believes in sharing wealth, we had created one of the largest stock option schemes in the country. SEBI Chennai's contention was that issuing shares to more than forty-nine employees in 2012 could be deemed as a public offer/issue under the Companies Act 1956. The Companies Act of 2013 specifically exempts issuance of shares to employees. Our counsel and bankers were clear that offering shares to employees for stock options cannot be considered a public issue.

SEBI Chennai firmly believed this was not the case and advised that we had to give an 'exit option' to our employees who got stocks in 2012. Since stocks were issued at Rs 2 per share, as the promotor I was required to make an offer to buy the shares at the princely amount of Rs 10 per share! Our bankers explained the absurdity of this since none of our employees had participated in the OFS. SEBI Chennai then told our bankers that the matter was being referred to the legal section in Mumbai. After three weeks we realized that no early relief would come from SEBI Mumbai. To avoid further delay, we agreed to go ahead with the exit process. We have no grudge against SEBI Chennai, as the dealing officer genuinely believed in his argument.

However, after we sent out the offer for Rs 10 per share to all employee shareholders and got 100 per cent regrets, the ever-vigilant officer in Chennai wanted copies of all the letters sent by us and an undertaking from me to redress grievances in the future. He also sent random messages to our employees to reconfirm that they'd received our offer and had declined the same. Some might feel that these further steps were well beyond the call of duty! Once all this was done, we were given a green signal to proceed with the IPO while applying to the registrar's office for condonation. The gentleman who received our condonation request asked, tongue in cheek, whether the promotor could not be accused of fraud for offering to buy the shares at Rs 10. The condonation application was accepted and will, no doubt, come up for adjudication in the future. We managed to complete the IPO ninety-nine days after the DRHP submission.

Why have I chosen to write about this experience in detail? Thanks to our own acquiescence, the precedent now is that any company which issued shares to more than forty-nine employees prior to the Companies Act 2013 will have to initiate an exit process and apply for condonation. Hopefully, SEBI or the Ministry of Corporate Affairs will issue a clarificatory notification that even prior to the 2013 Act, employees' shares for ESOP were exempt. Since ours was the first IPO initiated during the lockdown, we were helping to kick-start the primary market. We expected better support from the regulator, and this delay was therefore saddening.

Anchor Investors and Pricing of the Issue

Another new development since our MindTree IPO was the introduction of the concept of anchor investors. Seventy-five per cent of the book was reserved for qualified institutional buyers (QIB), of which 60 per cent is reserved for anchor investors. The system has merit because once good anchor investors come on board, the issue is assured of success. It does, however, give them and others who come through the main book a 'windfall' gain if the share prices take off after the listing, which is invariably the case.

Our experience regarding pricing the issue was also different from the MindTree instance. Then, our bankers had told us that the market would accept even a 25 per cent increase on our DRHP-indicated price, but we turned it down to give retail investors scope to get good returns. Here, we found the bankers exceedingly reluctant to increase even Rs 10 beyond Rs 166, the price we finally agreed upon.

We could only ascribe this to the desire to give anchor and main book investors a good deal, and also to the concern that some of them could back off, thereby jeopardizing the success of the IPO. To be fair to the bankers, pricing is an issue where you can't please everyone. For example, in the *Economic Times* there were two articles published on the same day—one said the issue was overpriced, the other accused us of 'mindless underpricing'.

The Aftermath of the Retail Frenzy

Markets have a way of overreacting. The retail frenzy for Happiest Minds led to a record listing-day increase. It also, inevitably, led to some course correction on the price, as a few of the anchor/main book investors and some retail investors decided to capture gains. Many retail investors come in late in the buying cycle, and I have no idea how to prevent this. These players see a price reduction due to correction and vent their frustration on platforms like Money Control. You need a thick skin to absorb their comments. Fortunately, there are as many who enjoin this group to hold on for the medium- and long-term. As I mentioned at the beginning of this chapter, we will assess the success of our IPO by the returns we deliver in a three-year time frame. We shall wait to be judged on this yardstick in due course. We have set ourselves a goal of delivering at least 10 per cent higher ROI than the average of leading industry players, which will be our benchmark for measuring our performance.

KEY TAKEAWAYS

✓ All the takeaways from the chapter titled 'Your Initial Public Offering' still hold good.

✓ Bankers have a long-term relationship with investors, while you will be their customers once or twice in a lifetime. They will, therefore, push you for maximum possible investor meetings.

✓ Investor roadshows done virtually are a huge source of time- and cost-saving. This should be made the de facto standard going forward even in a post-COVID world.

✓ In your investor presentations, please proactively bring up issues which may be the cause of uneasiness for investors, e.g. succession plan for me at Happiest Minds.

✓ The role of legal counsel in the IPO process has increased. All documents, presentations and statements have to be pre-approved by them.

✓ A target of ninety days from DRHP to listing is par for the course. You should try to shave off 5–10 days. However, be prepared for delays for unexpected reasons and from unexpected sources, such as SEBI in our case.

✓ If you have issued stocks to more than forty-nine employees prior to Companies Act 2013, you should approach SEBI early to clarify that this does not constitute a public issue. This should be done soon as you submit your DRHP. If approval doesn't come through in time, don't fight the system and go ahead with an exit process and condonation request.

✓ Anchor investors are important for the success of the issue. Getting their commitment is important. Bankers are likely to be influenced by their expectations while fixing the issue price.

✓ Heavy oversubscription will invariably be accompanied by a retail frenzy. Those who come in late will often express frustration on stock price, and you need a thick skin to endure their comments.

✓ Remain steadfast in your commitment that the success of the IPO should be judged by the returns delivered in a three-year time frame. Our goal is to give returns at least 10 per cent higher than the average of leading industry players.

Appendix

Of Critical Importance to Some

This section covers three different topics on which we often receive questions from the entrepreneurs we mentor. While these subjects are of critical importance to those specifically weighing out these issues, they may be of limited interest to others, which is why we have placed them in an appendix to the book.

The topics are:

- Whether one should opt for early-or late-stage entrepreneurship
- Serial entrepreneurship
- The opportunities and obstacles of entrepreneurship in the same space as your previous employer

Early- versus Late-stage Entrepreneurship

'The people who are crazy enough to think they can change the world are the ones who do'

—Steve Jobs

'You're never too old, never too bad, never too late and never too sick to start from scratch again'

—Bikram Choudhury

One of the questions we frequently get asked by young people just out of college is if it is too early for them to get into entrepreneurship. Likewise, older persons aged fifty and above have the query of whether it's too late.

The average experience profile of entrepreneurs is seven years. The age profile of the highest frequency for taking the entrepreneurial plunge is thirty-five to forty-five years, but there are large numbers of outliers on either side of those numbers. The high-profile success of several college dropouts, mostly in the US, has created a myth that entrepreneurs must be young, i.e. in their early to late twenties at the most. The list of college dropouts who made it big is a veritable who's who comprising Bill Gates, Steve Jobs, Mark Zuckerberg, Larry Ellison, Michael Dell, Travis Kalanick of Uber and Jan Koum of WhatsApp fame. The Google twins, Larry Page and Sergey Brin, were not dropouts, but they created the company while still studying at Stanford. The glamour of such young billionaire entrepreneurs has created a myth that entrepreneurs must be young, which can lead to a very unrealistic mindset in many others that they can replicate such success simply because they have age on their side. For each of these dramatic successes, there are hundreds of failed enterprises where the entrepreneurs were just not ready to cope with the challenges of entrepreneurship. It should also be remembered that the billionaire dropouts named above were brilliant individuals probably destined for greatness. The thesis of our book is that you don't have to be a genius to be a successful entrepreneur. Average, everyday persons can be successful entrepreneurs with the right mindset, the right experiences under their belt and by understanding the discipline of entrepreneurship.

In his book *Worthless, Impossible and Stupid*, Daniel Isenberg debunks the myth that entrepreneurs must be young. Of the fifteen entrepreneurial success stories covered in his book, eight feature entrepreneurs over forty and of these, three were over fifty at the time of starting their venture.

It's good to give a few examples of late-stage entrepreneurs here. Ashok started MindTree at the age of fifty-eight and Happiest Minds at sixty-nine. Dave Duffield started Workday at the age of sixty-four when PeopleSoft was acquired. Dr Paulraj, who started his career in the Indian navy, moved on to become a professor at Stanford and then started Beceem when he was fifty-nine-years-old. L.R. Sridhar was fifty-nine when he started Connect India. Of course, everyone's favourite example of a late-stage entrepreneur is Warren Buffet. At the age of eighty-three, he is still making new bets of an entrepreneurial nature every year, continuously transforming Berkshire Hathaway.

Keeping the above examples in mind, let's now see what works in favour of early-stage and late-stage entrepreneurs respectively. Early-stage entrepreneurs don't know what they don't know and therefore, are more likely to change the world. Also, they have an intuitive understanding of newer technologies which they use to build state-of-the-art offerings. They are also tuned to do a better job of exploiting social media to build a brand. What works against them is that in the excitement of entrepreneurship, they don't don their managerial and leadership hats until it's too late. Also, the lack of experience makes it more difficult for them to scale.

Coming to late-stage entrepreneurs, there is a unverified rumour that Palo Alto, the headquarters of the US venture industry, has a bias against age. We personally don't believe it's true and our profile of late-stage entrepreneurs indicates that one of their biggest advantages is that a good career track record helps in raising funds at a good valuation. This was certainly true for Ashok, and David Duffield was able to raise $175 million for Workday as well.

Late-stage entrepreneurs are likely to build on their past experience and therefore, are less likely to be new category creators. However, they usually adapt their experiences to create successful ventures. For example, L.R. Sridhar used his lifetime experience in logistics to connect rural India to the e-commerce network. Ashok built on his previous experiences to create Happiest Minds as a digital transformation enabling company. Best of all is Dave Duffield who used new cloud technologies to deliver his solution in the software-as-a-service model, thereby rendering obsolete the offerings of his prior company, PeopleSoft, which Oracle spent billions to acquire. There is another impression that older people lack the energy needed for an entrepreneurial venture. L.R. Sridhar was quoted in the *Economic Times* of 25 March 2016, saying, 'I am sixty-one now, but I work with the enthusiasm of a sixteen-year-old.' Ashok feels that it is his work and dealing with young people that keeps him engaged and energized. Though he has reduced his workload from a seventy-hour week to around sixty hours, he feels that the experience he has makes up in terms of effectiveness. It is only in an entrepreneurial mode that he can continue to work at the age of seventy-three.

Finally, we do believe that experience and track record not only help in securing funding and attracting talent, but seasoned and experienced entrepreneurs also bring in a wealth of relationships which can be leveraged for partnerships and building a customer base. Experience also helps in building an organization designed to scale. All these points have been true for Ashok at both MindTree and Happiest Minds and for many other late-stage entrepreneurs as well.

In summary, early-stage entrepreneurs are more likely to start greenfield ventures. The very successful amongst them will change the world, but this is a small percentage of such start-ups. The majority will face difficulties in scaling. Late-stage entrepreneurs are likely to build on their prior experiences. They may not create new product categories, but they have a much lower probability of failure.

Much of what we have said above are generalizations, and like all generalizations, only partly true. There are many examples to prove the opposite of some of our hypotheses. In conclusion, the right debate may not be that of early- versus late-stage entrepreneurship. The real issue is in terms of each individual's readiness for entrepreneurship. The right age and the right time for the entrepreneurial plunge is when *you* feel you are ready, *you* see the right opportunity, *you* are confident of funding the venture and attracting like-minded co-founders.

KEY TAKEAWAYS

✓ There is an increasingly developing myth that entrepreneurs have to be young. This is partly due to the high-profile entrepreneurial success stories of college dropouts mostly in the US. In reality, there are large number of entrepreneurs who start their ventures after the age of forty or fifty and some even after sixty.

- ✓ The young don't know what they don't know and are more likely to venture into the unknown and change the world. However, there are many more failed ventures started by youngsters as compared to those who bring in years of significant work experience.
- ✓ Experienced and late-stage entrepreneurs have a higher probability of success due to an ability to attract funds and talent based on their past track records. They also are better equipped to scale their enterprises and leverage their network for new partnerships and customers.
- ✓ The right age for entrepreneurship is when *you* are ready, *you* see the right opportunity, *you* are confident of funding the venture, attracting talent and building an organization.

Serial Entrepreneurship

'Ideas are like rabbits. You get a couple and learn how to handle them, and pretty soon you have a dozen'

—John Steinbeck

To the best of our knowledge, there is no formal classification of different types of serial entrepreneurs, what drives them and what they gain or lose through their different approaches to serial entrepreneurship. So, we will make a first-ever attempt to categorize serial entrepreneurs and identify their characteristics.

DNA-driven Serial Entrepreneurs

These are persons who have many ideas and get a big high out of starting something new. The two most prolific serial entrepreneurs of modern times that we can think of are Richard Branson in the UK and K. Ganesh in India.

While both Branson and Ganesh are prolific serial entrepreneurs, the similarity ends there. Branson has many visible ventures, some of which he has taken public. Virgin Air is perhaps the best known, but there is also Virgin Rail, Virgin Radio and Virgin Mobile. What is not widely known are the many failed enterprises created by Branson, which include Virgin Cola, Virgin Brides, Virgin Cars, Virginware, to mention a few. Most of Branson's successes have been in controlled and regulated markets where he was able to secure a beachhead and hold on to it.

In contrast, none of Ganesh's ventures has been a failure, but it would be fair to say that so far, they have all been moderate successes as their exits have yielded tens rather than hundreds of millions. Ganesh's ventures have varied widely from hardware maintenance to marketing in data analytics and TutorVista in edutech. In most of his recent start-ups, Ganesh has entered into areas which require digital marketing.

The most important difference between Branson and Ganesh is that Branson does not usually vacate a space that he enters and keeps adding to his empire as and when he starts a new venture. Also, there is a common brand across his ventures which itself has a value. Ganesh had been running only one company at a time until he and Meena Ganesh started their entrepreneurial platform where they now have multiple ventures with different CEOs. Ganesh has been clear that he does not want to run a public company, hence the continuous exits through strategic sales. However, this may be about to change. Meena, his nuts-and-bolts partner, is CEO of Portea and is reputedly keen on taking both Portea and BigBasket public. Both companies have scaled well and acquired leadership positions in new sunrise industries.

We have chosen two entrepreneurs with opposing objectives to showcase how DNA-driven serial entrepreneurs are wired. There are, of course, many more. Jawad Ayaz and Krishna Lakamsani have both done four ventures each and are young enough to have several more in them in their lives ahead. They are both serial entrepreneurs cast from the Ganesh mould—i.e. they create ventures, sell them and move on to the next. The primary characteristic of this breed is that they get bored or restless after a few years. They also feel that their maximum contribution is in the first seven to eight years of a venture and further scaling an organization is better left to someone else.

An interesting variation of the DNA-driven serial entrepreneur is the failed entrepreneur who is determined to try and try again until he or she succeeds. Apparently, Silicon Valley VCs have a great preference for failed entrepreneurs because of their determination to succeed. We have no confirmatory evidence and this may just be one of the myths of the entrepreneurial world. If it is true that the failed entrepreneur has great fortitude, would the opposite also be true—that a highly successful entrepreneur may have less motivation? Since we see serial entrepreneurs as DNA-driven, we feel that motivation and the drive to succeed remains high even after repeated success. The danger lies in a sense of hubris that they can do no wrong and also in not realizing that what worked previously may not work the next time round as markets and challenges change.

Accidental or Event-driven Serial Entrepreneurs

In this category of entrepreneurs, whose serial entrepreneurship arose due to an event, we would include Dave Duffield and Ashok. It's unlikely that Dave would have set up Workday if he had not lost PeopleSoft through a hostile acquisition. Ashok first took a decision to move on from MindTree due to internal happenings and only later decided to create his new company, Happiest Minds. Ashok can say for himself (which probably applies to Dave as well) that what looked like a catastrophic event turned out to be the best thing that ever happened to him.

Technology Experts Building on a Unique Expertise

In this category of serial entrepreneurs, we would include Dr Paulraj of Stanford and Prem Jain of Cisco.

Paul's career in the Indian navy was an unlikely start for a serial entrepreneur. After building the navy's anti-submarine sonar and setting up three labs for the Indian government, Paul moved to Stanford University. There, he pioneered a breakthrough technology called MIMO (multiple input, multiple output) that dramatically increases the data rate of wireless systems. Despite wide scepticism about MIMO, Paul founded Iospan Wireless in 1998 to build MIMO for the next generation (4G) cellular systems. Later, in 2003, at age fifty-nine, he co-founded Beceem Communications to focus on 4G semiconductors. Paul understood that inserting a new technology into large ecosystems like that of the mobile wireless needed companies with significant financial muscle. Accordingly, he sold Iospan to Intel and Beceem to Broadcom.

Likewise, Prem Jain, a brilliant engineer, realized that his skill lay in creating new products but it was not his forte to run companies and scale them to their potential. He sold his first company to Cisco. Later, along with a few other colleagues, he stepped out of Cisco to start Nuova Systems. In the pressure-cooker atmosphere of a start-up, they were able to develop a next generation server and a switching product, found an eager acquirer in Cisco again, where the product soon became a billion dollar-plus category. This approach was so successful that Prem and his friends repeated it by starting Insieme Networks and again finding a ready suitor at Cisco. Even as we wrote this, Prem and his three friends have again resigned from Cisco. Their future plans are yet to be announced, but we would not be surprised if these include another venture.

Upstream or Downstream Diversifiers

Entrepreneurs in this category understand the entire vertical supply chain and value drivers of their industry so well that upstream or downstream serial entrepreneurship is the logical way to go for them. The most celebrated upstream entrepreneur of India, and probably the world, is Dhirubhai

Ambani, who created India's largest company, Reliance Industries. He began his entrepreneurial journey in the mature and unglamorous textile industry. He established leadership by becoming a pioneer in synthetic textiles when synthetic yarns first appeared. His first upstream effort was to set up plants for the manufacture of polyester yarns. In a country where production capacity was mindlessly restricted by industrial licences, he was the first to create world-scale plants. His next move was to set up petrochemical plants which produced the raw materials for these yarns. The final upstream thrust was to enter into the oil industry, which was the source for the petrochemicals. The last effort was driven by his son Mukesh, who inherited his ability to implement ventures on a world-class and world-scale basis.

A great example of downstream diversification is V.G. Siddhartha. Siddhartha began as a coffee producer and for many years enhanced his capacity by acquiring plantations around his home base of Chikmagalur in Karnataka. At that time, all marketing of coffee in India went through the Coffee Board. When coffee marketing was thrown open, he entered into coffee exports and soon became India's number one coffee exporter. Finally, to increase the realization on his product, he entered the retail segment through Café Coffee Day. Notwithstanding the travails of the stock shortly after the IPO, Siddhartha remains optimistic. He points out that Starbucks went public in 1992 at $200 million and is now valued at $90 billion. Café Coffee Day went public at $1 billion and is firmly entrenched with its vast retail network and a country where per store sales are increasing rapidly. A lesser known upstream entrepreneurial approach of Siddhartha's is his leasing of a forest in Guyana to support his furniture business. Both his coffee and furniture business are outside the ambit of his holding company, which he has taken public.

New Genre-creating Serial Entrepreneurs

Genre-creating serial entrepreneurs are what Isenberg describes in his book as people who can see what no others can. This category of entrepreneur raises the bar for the rest of us as it's extremely difficult to create a new category or a new genre of industry. The most successful and best-known entrepreneur in this category is Steve Jobs and both his name and story are forces unto himself, which need no further explanation.

Another example we would like to cite is that of Deidre Paknad, co-founder of Workboard. Her previous venture, PSS Systems, since acquired by IBM, invented a new category of software when it anticipated the challenges companies would face when expanding legal requirements for information collided with extreme information volumes. She developed the first commercial application for legal holds, collection and retention management by creating linkages across legal records and IT. An ability to invent, not just innovate, seems to be a characteristic of such entrepreneurs which enables the creation of new categories. Not surprisingly, Deidre has sixteen patents in total, either issued or pending!

The greatest and most prolific inventor-cum-serial entrepreneur of all time was Thomas Edison, whose invention included the electric light bulb, but his invention also influenced electric utilities, the phonograph and a motion picture camera. Many of his inventions are still a part of GE's current offerings.

KEY TAKEAWAYS

✓ Serial entrepreneurs can be of different varieties. Some are DNA-driven, others have unique technology expertise which can have multiple practical applications, some are upstream or downstream diversifiers, some have the capability of creating new genres in industries and, finally, some are accidental or event-driven serial entrepreneurs. All of them build on capabilities derived from their past experiences.

✓ Many serial entrepreneurs sell their ventures before moving on to the next, while others continue to run most or all of the enterprises they start and thereby build an empire. Those who exit their ventures may give up much of the potential market capitalization which tends to grow sharply between eight to twelve years of a successful venture as the hockey stick effect kicks in. An exit can still be the right decision for such entrepreneurs if they feel they don't have the ability or resources to grow the organization to its potential.

✓ Serial entrepreneurs can include those who have failed in their past efforts or those who have always been and usually are successful.

Entrepreneurship in the Same Space as Your Previous Employer

'Tread softly because you tread on my dreams'

—W.B. Yeats

It is not unlikely that an experienced leader will choose to build on prior experience by starting a company in the same space as his or her previous employer. Experience in a particular industry is undoubtedly useful but to be successful, one has to ensure a new approach in the new venture as well. We found this to be true for the three entrepreneurs we cite as examples in this section.

Vardaan Vasisht began his career at Accenture and then joined a start-up in the US in the digital advertising space named Beyond Interactive. After Beyond Interactive went through two acquisitions, he started HookLogic, also in the digital media space, but created it as a digital media platform. We have already illustrated earlier how Dave Duffield changed the business and delivery model while starting a company in the same space he had worked previously in.

Bill Draper in his book, *The Start-up Game*, says if a senior manager of a successful enterprise leaves to start a similar or related-space enterprise, it does improve the probability of the new venture being successful, provided there are no ethical issues involved in the venture and it has everyone's blessings. We agree entirely with Bill on the ethical aspects, which we see as imperative. However, we disagree on the aspect of having 'everyone's blessings'. The company the entrepreneur leaves behind is bound to be concerned about its loss of key people and customers. Far from blessing you, they may threaten legal action to try to stall you or intimidate you.

The problems will generally come from non-compete or non-solicit clauses in the contract. It should be noted that many countries or states in the US don't recognize non-compete clauses as legal. In India too there are legal judgements against the non-compete clause which is, therefore, not enforceable. An important point to note on both the non-compete and non-solicit clauses is that any such activity during the course of employment would be illegal and any action on approaching existing employees or customers is not permitted until after the employment has ceased and the entrepreneur has stepped out of the company.

During Ashok's Wipro days, there were no non-compete or non-solicit clauses in the employee contracts, and these were introduced only after Ashok's departure. When Ashok's co-founders (at MindTree) approached him, he realized there were three others from his previous team among them. As a matter of abundant precaution, he informed the chairman of this development which came within a week of his resignation being accepted. Ashok also took the precaution that henceforth, there would be no more approaching of others at Wipro until Ashok had officially left after completing the six months' notice he had given for finding a successor. But, as Ashok puts it:

In spite of ensuring that everything was done correctly, I was surprised that shortly after starting MindTree, we were shown a legal notice drafted by a high-profile legal firm in California threatening action for hiring Wipro persons. We were further informed that this notice would be issued if we continued with any hiring. I bought a month's time, during which I said we would make no further offers. In this period, I visited the US and met with lawyers who assured us we needn't have any concerns. Thereafter, I briefed our investors and secured their support. This was followed by an eyeball-to-eyeball confrontation, in which we literally invited the lawsuit saying we would file our own countersuit. However, I added that we were keen on diversifying our talent base and would voluntarily restrict our hiring for the first year to fifty-two persons, approximately 20 per cent of our expected strength. We never heard anything further on legal action and honoured this informal offer.

The situation in the transition from MindTree to Happiest Minds was even stranger, indeed curious. Around November 2010, I had decided to move on from MindTree, but had not announced my intentions to even my co-founders. I was contemplating different options and asked the CFO if an NGO which did pro bono IT projects for the government would violate my non-compete clause. To my pleasant surprise, he responded that, in February 2011, four years after our IPO, all our non-compete clauses would drop away. Accordingly, I decided that I should do my new venture in an area I understood well. Several months later, when I made my surprise resignation announcement, in response to media queries, the same CFO and the CEO & MD together responded that I was bound by both the non-compete and non-solicit!

Realizing that this erroneous statement could later on create fear, uncertainty and doubt in the minds of potential employees and customers, I demanded a letter from the CEO & MD that I was not covered by any non-compete or non-solicit agreements. We even issued a joint press release whereby MindTree acknowledged that I had the freedom to hire a few employees and also compete in existing customer accounts. In return, I gave them a letter saying I would not sell my shares in a way that would jeopardize or create difficulty for the management.

In spite of all the above, it did not deter MindTree from intimidating and sending legal letters to persons who joined me, and also filing a legal case in the US. The intimidation was directed at my chief people officer and the first twenty-three persons who joined Happiest Minds for violating non-compete provisions. The letters were absurd and all the situation needed was a strong rejoinder to put an end to this nonsense; we continued to selectively hire a few of the many MindTree persons who approached us.

Then, a formal legal case was filed in the US against the president of one of the Happiest Minds business units and his country sales head, for calling on and making bids for an account which was then MindTree's largest account and today, the largest account by far. There really was no case and MindTree dithered and delayed responses to our rejoinder. After eighteen months, we were able to have the suit dismissed with recovery of all legal costs; and yet, Happiest Minds was hurt as we will show below.

What are the lessons to be learned from these experiences? First, that you have to be very, very cautious in observing the letter and spirit of the law. Then, if any legal action comes your way, don't allow yourself to be intimidated and confront the issue head-on. A threat of a countersuit can help. Ashok didn't speak to a single MindTree person to join him at his new venture, including his future co-founders, until after he left the company. Secondly, you should be prepared for the company you are leaving to behave in a paranoid and even irrational way to intimidate your start-up. Customers don't switch easily to a new entity as they develop links at different levels with the operating company, and so this anxiety is somewhat misplaced. Even five years after Ashok's departure, MindTree's top two customers are accounts where Ashok's relationships and front-end involvements played a key role in winning the same.

Though you should be well placed to confront threats of legal action, it doesn't mean that you will not have some damage inflicted even if you get the suit dismissed with the full reimbursement of legal costs, as happened with us in the case of MindTree. Ashok had to personally brief the lawyer in India and also personally select the legal counsel in the US and approve all defence communications. As a start-up founder, he could not take any risk of things going awry and besides, he was the only one who had the complete background on the non-compete and non-solicit clauses and understood their nuances. This was a diversion of valuable time away from business development. Furthermore, the US sales head was so concerned about being a defendant in a legal suit that he stopped making sales calls to a large potential customer. Within a year, he left the company, setting back the account entry approach by a few years. In the larger context, the above actions were obstacles but only a blip in Happiest Minds' path towards creating a successful company. Ashok would also like to clarify that he continues to have cordial relations with his past co-founders at MindTree as they have a shared warm memory of creating an excellent company together.

Legal hurdles and other obstacles can come from not only your former employers, but also partners or large players in the space you are entering. Mårten Mickos, CEO of MySQL in Sweden, in its early days recalls that just as he was taking charge, they were hit by a double whammy. They were sued by their former partner in the US for unfair trade practices, amongst other things. MySQL's response was to gain the support of their VCs and file a countersuit. Later, the matter was closed by an out-of-court settlement. Shortly after this, Oracle suddenly acquired one of MySQL's key partners, InnoDB. They were devastated because a vital component of their product was now owned by their largest competitor. Martin and his team decided that an attack was the best defence. They built a marketing campaign featuring the company's dolphin logo with a message that trying to kill MySQL by buying InnoDB was 'like trying to kill a dolphin by drinking the ocean'. This powerful message led to huge developer support for MySQL and a problem was converted into an opportunity. More brittle founding teams may have given up and not risen up to the battle. The lesson is that entrepreneurs must take such challenges in their stride and gain greater strength by overcoming them.

KEY TAKEAWAYS

✓ It's likely that your previous company will have concerns regarding the loss of people or customers if your new venture is in the same space as them. In such circumstances, you should be prepared that they may create obstacles in your path, which usually come in the form of legal suits on non-compete or non-solicit clauses.

✓ You have to be absolutely sure that you have followed the commitments of your employment contract in letter and spirit and also the law of the land in every respect. India, like many countries and most states in the US, does not accept non-compete clauses as legal. There may be some exceptions against joining select named competitors, but definitely no bars against your starting up in the same space. The non-compete clause does apply if you are still in employment and solicit potential employees. Therefore, conversations to attract people should be put on hold until after you have formally left the company.

✓ Apart from previous employers, obstacles and legal action can also come from other large players in the industry. This could include having one of your key product or channel partners acquired.

✓ You should always be mentally prepared for hostile or legal actions. When something adverse does happen, the first response is to secure the support of your investors and then confront the challenge head-on. This could include a countersuit if the charges against you are frivolous and not based on law. Even when you win, you will be impacted as your valuable time has gone into legal defence instead of building the business. Still, this is the preferred approach instead of being brittle and succumbing to the attack. The ideal outcome will be if you can convert the problem into an opportunity.

Top Takeaways

'The best way to predict the future is to create it'

—Peter Drucker

Entrepreneurship is all about creating the future. We hope that *Entrepreneurship Simplified* has shown you the path to the future all the way from idea generation to the IPO and beyond. We have drawn up key takeaways at the end of each chapter. Though we believe that each of these chapters is relevant for your success, we would like to close this book by summarizing the top takeaways for your quick and ready reference.

✓ Your venture is only as good as your idea. Accordingly, evaluate multiple opportunities before you settle on the one for your venture. Idea generation methods can include the kaleidoscope approach.

✓ Your chosen idea must solve a customer's pain, be a new way of delivering an existing service or disrupt existing businesses. You must put your idea through an inexpensive validation test, including proof of concept checks for scalability and defensibility.

✓ We have a strong preference for raising funds from external sources rather than bootstrapping. Money is the fuel for accelerated growth scaling. Also, VCs validate your idea and add value.

✓ You should have a strategy for all the fundraising cycles till the pre-IPO round. Work backwards and decide on the money to be raised per round. The objective should be to maximize valuation at each stage and minimize dilution. Equity once given away can't be recovered.

✓ Before negotiating with VCs, understand their minds, imperatives and drivers. Is the money they provide 'intelligent money'? Don't just accept the first offer you receive.

✓ Entrepreneurship is about value creation, and you need to ensure that the founders capture their fair share of value creation. You target should be that the founders retain a minimum 40 per cent and preferably 50 per cent or above of shareholding in the pre-IPO round.

✓ Shareholder agreements can contain onerous clauses. You need professional help to negotiate these agreements. In a rush to get money, don't agree to clauses which give the VCs the right to replace the CEO or clauses which can restrict your operational freedom. The entrepreneur–VC relationship is mostly cordial and supportive. However, things can turn sour, and you need to protect yourself.

✓ Organizational culture can be your most unique and enduring differentiator which others can't easily replicate.

✓ Mission, vision and values (MVV) play an important role in defining the type of culture you want to create. The MVV must be consistent with each other and should be simple, inspirational and aspirational. For this to translate into reality, the MVV must be well internalized and senior leaders must be role models.

✓ It is best to avoid M&A activity for the first three to four years of a company's life. Different companies have different cultures, even though some will appear to be similar. A 'too early' M&A is like grafting another culture on to your own even before it has taken firm root.

✓ Don't just call your company and team a family without being able to demonstrate the same through the way you behave, particularly in difficult times.

✓ Building your organization begins with creating the right foundation, the responsibility for which rests with the founders. There are no guidelines to help you ascertain whether two founders or many more are right for your venture. We don't recommend a single-founder set-up, and VCs also tend to frown upon it. It is important to have complementarity in founders' capabilities. If not, there is a tendency to force-fit people into roles.

✓ Equity sharing between founders need not be equal or egalitarian, but should be broadly in proportion to expected value addition.

✓ Founders should come in expecting and receiving a salary cut as the start-up won't be able to afford their prior salaries. The senior-most founders and those who receive the highest equity should take the largest salary cuts. High founder salaries are a red flag for VCs.

✓ Being a founder is not a role, neither is it an entitlement for any special concessions. Accordingly, if a founder is not measuring up, he or she should be treated like any other member of the team: provide maximum support and if things still don't work out, plan for a separation.

✓ The most important role in the company is that of the CEO. The one amongst the founders who is clearly seen as the leader should be the CEO.

- ✓ The organization structure is not so much about hierarchies or reporting relationships, but it defines your go-to-market approach, operational efficiency and accountability. Your profit centres will determine your organization's power structure.
- ✓ The opportunity cost of a wrong hire is five times the direct cost until separation. Accordingly, it's better for leaders to multitask and fill the gap than hire in haste.
- ✓ You need a continuum of strategies, including a start-up strategy, a scale-up strategy, a strategy to compete against much larger players, a strategy to pivot if required, a strategy for risk reduction and a strategy for acquisition. For every inflection point in your company or major externally induced change, you need to revisit your strategy.
- ✓ Price is not a strategy; it's a mug's game. Market entry at lower prices is only justified if your costs are lower, allowing you to sustain healthy margins.
- ✓ Platformization of your offerings is a great tool to scale both B2B and B2C markets. In B2B, it can yield annuity business in the form of multi-year contracts. In B2C, it helps you to enlarge your reach and lower your customer acquisition costs. Platforms can help you make money while you sleep.
- ✓ You can successfully compete against large companies as they all have their own weaknesses. Techniques you can use include guerilla tactics, judo strategy and Tai Chi thinking.
- ✓ Every strategy is only as good as its implementation. Good execution requires working backwards from the three- or five-year vision and drawing up a road map of actions.

- ✓ The best publicity is free publicity. Third-party statements, such as media articles and social media comments, have higher credibility than your own declarations or paid advertisements. Customer testimonials provide the most powerful publicity. To get a vast amount of free coverage, 'be interesting, do interesting'.
- ✓ Building trust is important in both B2B and B2C marketing. When things go wrong, handle these exceptions well as they can contribute to how trustworthy you appear.
- ✓ Excessive choice in pricing, schemes and variety can confuse a customer and lead to delays in decision-making. Keep it simple. The future of marketing lies in improving the customer's experience and demonstrating that you care. Those who do this well will be the winners.
- ✓ We recommend a generous and all-inclusive ESOP scheme. You will have many priorities when you start a company, but it's important to develop your ESOP scheme even as you are preparing to launch your venture. You need to be aware of taxability provisions which vary from country to country and also change from time to time. It's best to distribute founder sweat equity before the company becomes operational and also disburse a significant proportion of your ESOP pool earlier rather than later.
- ✓ Strategic sale of a venture is the most common exit route for founders and also for investors. Reason being that most organizations cannot build adequate scale and predictability of growth/profitability to do an IPO. For founders, the sale of the venture is an emotive decision. There will be happiness and a strong sense of loss.

- ✓ It is okay to start a company with the objective of selling the same, but only if you remain focused on creating value.

- ✓ The best propositions for getting high value from a strategic sale are when you have created intellectual property, be it a product or platform. Valuation will also be high if your company fulfils a strategic objective for the buyer. Good corporate governance will always get you a valuation premium.

- ✓ The standard rules for enterprise valuation do not apply to a strategic sale. The valuation should be based on what the acquirer can achieve with the acquisition and the strategic objectives it fulfils for the acquirer. The keys to a good price are the IPs and capabilities you have built and the future-proofing of your platform/product. It's good to aim for the moon in a strategic sale.

- ✓ An IPO requires years of advance planning. This includes action on governance and disclosure requirements of the Companies Act and stock exchange listing agreements, which become applicable to you as a public limited company. About twelve to eighteen months before your IPO, you should expand the board to meet the requirements of having the necessary proportion of independent directors. Select directors who bring in complementary capabilities and who can add value.

- ✓ The key decisions for the IPO are the size of issue, the price of issue and the valuation of the company. Your investment banker will help you finalize these, but you need to be aware that too many stocks tend to be below issue price even a few years after the IPO. We define a successful IPO as one which gives good returns to existing investors and also new investors as measured over a three-year time frame.

✓ Ventures started by young entrepreneurs are more likely to attempt to change the world, but also have a higher failure rate. Late-stage entrepreneurs are likely to build on their past experiences, which makes it easier for them to raise funds, attract talent and scale the venture.

✓ Serial entrepreneurs are broadly of two types: those who move from venture to venture, and others who retain control of their prior ventures and create an empire. Paths towards serial entrepreneurship vary depending on which skills the serial entrepreneur seeks to leverage.

✓ If you start a venture in the same space as your previous employer, you may have to face legal suits on non-compete or non-solicit clauses. You should be aware of the law and ensure you are on the right side of it. Don't be intimidated and take a head-on approach to confront such situations.

✓ Failure and success are two ends of the spectrum. At the low end are situations where you have to shut shop or make a distress sale. In between are ventures with varying degrees of under- and overperformance. At the top end are ventures with excellent financial success, good corporate governance and a sustainable business model for the future.

✓ An important factor for success is to get your timing right all the way from idea selection, market entry, scale-up, to pivoting strategy, if needed, and acquisition, etc. You have to find the right timing in an environment of uncertainty.

✓ The two biggest reasons for venture failure are 'no market need' and 'ran out of cash'. A single huge mistake can lead to venture failure. On the other hand, to be on the high end of the success spectrum, you need to skilfully implement innumerable acts well all the way from planning to execution. This covers the entire gamut of areas, from idea generation to IPO and beyond. In addition, you will need multiple personal attributes like perseverance, flexibility, agility and resilience to sustain your goals for the future.

✓ You should be passionate about your venture, but don't get consumed by it and let it destroy your personal life. Apart from achieving financial success, entrepreneurship should be a happy and joyous journey and a journey filled with purpose to be called truly successful.

Glossary

acquisition Purchase of one business enterprise by another.

addressable market Revenue opportunity available for a product or service as a portion of the total market.

advisory board An invited group of experts that provides non-binding strategic advice to management.

angel investors Individual investors who provide financial backing for small start-ups or entrepreneurs.

anti-dilution A provision in a shareholders' agreement which protects the investor if the issuer sells new securities at a lower price.

attrition rate Employee turnover expressed as a percentage of the total number of employees, usually described as an annualized number.

B2B Business-to-business transactions or business model.

B2C Business-to-consumer transactions or business model.

B2B2C An acronym for 'business-to-business-to-consumer', it is an emerging e-commerce model that addresses the consumer market through a B2B channel.

bootstrapping A situation in which an entrepreneur builds a company with personal capital, generally a small amount.

BPO Business Process Outsourcing.

break even The amount of revenue from sales which exactly equals the amount of expenses.

BU Business Unit.

build-operate-transfer (BOT) A type of arrangement in which a service provider builds a project, operates it and eventually transfers ownership of the project to the company for whom the arrangement was agreed upon. (This often includes transfer of the team which was earlier generating revenue for the service provider.)

cash flow The amount of actual cash generated by business operations, which usually differs from book profits, the difference being non-cash expenses such as depreciation are included in the latter.

corporate governance A system of rules, practices and processes by which a company is directed and controlled for the benefit of shareholders, with the board of directors at the apex.

crowdsourcing The practice of obtaining services, ideas, funds or content by soliciting contributions from a large group of people and especially from the online community rather than from traditional investors, employees or suppliers.

dilution for ESOPs When new shares are issued against the ESOP, the stake of existing owners gets diluted.

drag-along rights Rights that enable an investor to force other shareholders to join in the sale of shares.

due diligence An investigation of the enterprise undertaken by professional advisors on behalf of the purchaser of or financial investor in a business.

earn-out shares A pricing structure in mergers and acquisitions where the sellers must 'earn' part of the purchase price based on the performance of the business following the acquisition.

egalitarian sharing The principle that all founders are more or less equal and deserve an equal or similar share of equity.

equity The owners' share of a business.

ERP Enterprise Resource Planning.

escrow account A temporary pass-through account held by a third party during the process of a transaction between two parties.

ESOP (Employee Stock Option Plan) A type of employee benefit plan which is intended to encourage employees to acquire stocks or ownership in the company.

exit strategy A way of 'cashing out' an investment.

gestation period The period of time between a business idea or plan and its implementation.

glass door ratings A website on which current and former employees anonymously review companies and their management.

gorilla competition Competition against giant competitors.

go-to-market approach An action plan that specifies how a company will reach customers and achieve competitive advantage.

GPTW (Great Place to Work) The Great Place to Work® Institute is a firm that helps organizations create great workplaces by developing cultures built on trust.

gross margins The difference between revenue and cost of goods sold.

GTV Global Technology Ventures.

hockey stick effect A description of the graphic shape of a line chart which resembles a hockey stick; the line shows a sharp rise in performance after a flat period.

hyperlocal A very specific area or community.

incubation centre A company that helps new and start-up companies to develop by providing services such as research, management training or office space.

intellectual property (IP) Intangible property that is the result of creativity, such as patents, copyrights, etc.

Internet of things (IoT) A system of interrelated computing devices, mechanical and digital machines, objects, animals or people that are provided with unique identifiers and the ability to transfer data over a network without requiring human-to-human or human-to-computer interaction.

IPO (Initial Public Offering) The sale of shares to the public by a company for the first time.

kaleidoscope approach A kaleidoscope is a toy consisting of a tube where rotations produce continuously changing patterns; a kaleidoscope approach, articulated for the first time by Ashok Soota, is a methodology to generate new ideas and business models.

legal hold Legal hold is a process that an organization uses to preserve all forms of relevant information when litigation is reasonably anticipated.

liquidation preference A term used in venture capital agreements to specify which investors get paid first and how much they get paid in the event of a liquidation event such as the sale of the company; it determines how the selling price is shared on a liquidity event.

M & A Mergers and Acquisitions.

market capitalization/market cap Aggregate valuation of the company based on its current share price and the total number of outstanding stocks.

market share The portion of a market controlled by a particular company or product.

market size A measurement of the total volume of a given market in revenue terms.

MIMO Multiple Input, Multiple Output.

MSME Micro, small and medium enterprises.

NASSCOM National Association of Software and Services Companies.

ODM (Original Design and Manufacturing)/OEM (Original Equipment Manufacturer) A company that designs or makes a part or subsystem that is used in another company's end product.

opportunity cost The loss of other alternatives when one alternative is chosen.

participative rights The right to share pro rata in the liquidation proceeds in addition to liquidation preference.

platform A combination of hardware, software, data and technologies using which a system or an application can be developed easily as opposed to ground-up development.

Product Engineering Service (PES) The process of designing and developing a software, device, assembly or system such that it be produced as an item for sale.

profit centre A part of an organization with assignable revenues and costs and hence ascertainable profitability.

razor-blade pricing strategy The razor/razor-blade model has evolved to mean any business practice in which a company offers a one-time product at minimal or low cost to drive the sale of another product for which the consumer is required to make repeated purchases.

red flag An indicator of potential problems.

revenue multiple Enterprise value divided by its revenue; a revenue multiple measures the value of the equity or a business relative to the revenues that it generates.

ROI (Return on Investment) Measures the amount of return on an investment relative to the investment's cost; this is expressed in percentage terms.

SaaS Software as a Service.

serial entrepreneur An entrepreneur who starts more than one new venture.

sweat equity Equity that is given to the founder of the company in recognition of the effort expended in establishing the business.

tag-along If a shareholder sells his or her stake, then the other shareholders with tag-along right (typically investors) are entitled to join the transaction and sell their stake in the company.

TiE The Indus Entrepreneurs.

unicorn companies A start-up company that gets valued at over $1 billion in a short period of time.

valuation The process of determining the current worth of an asset, business or company.

VC Venture capitalist.

VC circle An online data platform with information on VC/PE/ M & A deals, deal multiples, IPOs, etc.

vesting period The time that an employee must wait in order to be able to exercise options (ESOPs).

veto A right that ensures that certain important actions cannot take place in the company without the approval of the investors.

virgin territory Ideas, concepts or activities that have not yet been tried, explored or developed.

VLSI (Very Large Scale Integration) The process of creating an integrated circuit by combining thousands of transistors into a single chip.

white label basis A product or service produced by one company (the producer) that other companies (the marketers) rebrand and take to market under their own label.